I am fifteen – and I don't want to die...

by CHRISTINE ARNOTHY

SCHOLASTIC BOOK SERVICES

NEW YORK·TORONTO·LONDON·AUCKLAND·SYDNEY·TOKYO

Only fifteen when she lived through the events told about in this book, Christine Arnothy left Hungary four years later, in 1948. While she was living in Belgium and writing this story from the diaries she had kept during the siege of Budapest, Christine was working in a bookstore.

"Nobody knew," she writes, "that I would rather write books than sell them." *I Am Fifteen—and I Don't Want To Die* won the Prix de Verites (French prize for nonfiction) the year it was published.

ISBN: 0-590-02528-7

Copyright © 1956 by E. P. Dutton & Co., Inc. This edition is published by Scholastic Book Services, a division of Scholastic Magazines, Inc., by arrangement with E. P. Dutton & Co., Inc.

25 24 23 22 21 20   1/8

Printed in the U.S.A.

06

1.

CHAPTER

Pista came that evening like a deliverer. It was almost night, although we could not tell night from day, buried as we were in the mildewed cellar of an apartment house on the edge of the Danube.

Nevertheless, our watches serenely kept on registering the time; the hands ticked calmly around the dials. Was it for two weeks or for two years that we had been living like moles?

Would there ever be again a "today," and a "tomorrow," or just an eternity of dark, smoky cellars?

The first three days had passed fairly quickly. At each creak of the stairs, we thought: Here come the Russians; the fighting in this district is over; we can go up to our rooms again and pick up the threads of our lives just where they had snapped — finish reading the half-read book, go on playing the sonata that still lay open on the piano, reopen the notebook with the blue paper cover and complete that assignment in Hungarian composition.

On the fifth day of our exile underground, it became evident that the Germans had decided to defend the city. It was then that we lost all notion of time. The empty, anxious days followed each other with oppressive slowness. The mobile A.A. gun, barking incessantly in front of the house, drew danger down on our heads. The little gun mounted on a truck could not do much harm to the enemy planes: it could do little more than irritate them. It would fire a salvo or two, then flee and begin its little game a street or two farther away, only to return again. The heavy Russian planes passed over the houses in a roar of thunder and dropped their bombs at random, searching for the enemy that played hide-and-seek with them. In this sinister game of blindman's buff it was we who wore the blindfold! With our eyes shut and our faces buried in our hands, we listened tensely to the passing planes and, from time to time, our trembling fingers anxiously touched the sweating walls. Could these stones withstand such violent blows forever?

The tenants of the house who had lived their

separate lives without knowing one another, now found themselves all crammed together in the same cellar. Here they slept, ate, washed, and squabbled in complete promiscuity. The majority of them had staked their claim in the main cellar, which had been shored up with stout props when it was converted into an air-raid shelter. But these beams seemed to offer no more protection than a row of toothpicks against the battle that raged above us.

We had chosen a small cellar a little farther away in which, in peacetime, we had stored our coal. In this sooty, smelly place now stood two beds, a couch and a table. In the beginning we had had a little stove with a chimney which let the smoke out through a ventilator opening into the courtyard. But very soon we had to give up this heating system, for at night sparks escaping from the iron stovepipe offered a target to the enemy.

The town was burning all around us while we shivered on our heap of coal. We used to bring water from Duck Street; by some strange chance there was a tap there that had not run dry. From the first day, we had no electricity. We put some cooking fat in a shoe-polish can with a shoelace as a wick. This evil-smelling candle gave a wan, yellowish light.

The janitor and his wife had settled in the small cellar next to ours. She was a tall, stout woman accustomed to big tips; he, a puny little man with a dead-white face and shifty eyes. Their son lived in the neighborhood of the Citadel and had recently married. He worked for the firm where his father had been a doorman for twenty years. Jancsi's parents had succeeded in making him into an "intellectual," and a "gentleman;" he was their great pride. They had plenty of food, and felt no lack of water for they drank wine.

The little cellar next to ours on the other side sheltered Ilus and her baby. She was about thirty-six. Lovely fair hair framed her tiny, faded doll's face. As her eyebrows were colorless, she darkened them with a piece of charcoal. She never forgot to do this, even in the worst air raids. Her husband had deserted her a few weeks ago, leaving Ilus alone with her six-month-old baby. Her parents lived in the city but she lacked the courage to make her way through the torrents of shrapnel to join them on the other bank of the Danube.

There was also a medical student whom everyone called "Doctor." As he was only in his second year at medical school, this began by being merely a joke, but the title stuck to him. It reassured people to tell each other that, if anything happened, they had a doctor at hand. This undersized youth, whose face was covered with freckles, looked like a schoolboy, but now that he realized his presence had a calming effect, he put on airs.

4

The student's aunt was the widow of a banker. She was a plump little woman, as neat and shining as a new coin. She spent her time lamenting her fate and wondering whether all her securities would be safe in her strongbox at the bank. She wore her jewels in a little bag hung around her neck. The banker, her husband, had died before the war after some quite ordinary illness. But his worthy spouse so emphatically stressed the noble part he would have played were he still alive, that he was about to become a hero who had fallen on the field of honor. This dear lady poked her nose into everything, inspected and tasted everybody's cooking, asked and gave advice, and constantly talked about herself. When the men hesitated to brave the showers of melted snow and shrapnel to go for the water, she cried: "If my dear Albert were still alive, *he'd* go at once. He was afraid of nothing!"

"The Colonel's Lady" was a heavily built woman. During the air bombardment that preceded the siege of Budapest, chance had made her an air-raid warden. Her loud voice was the source of her power; she wanted to give orders to everyone. She often made the rounds of the cellar for no apparent reason, just to keep track of things. Her political opinions were vague since she did not know whether her husband, the colonel, was still fighting the Russians or whether he had joined the resistance. Sometimes the colonel was presented in the role of legendary hero defending the city with his last drop of blood. At other times he appeared as the liberator of Budapest. In actual fact, he was probably a prisoner of one side or the other, but this possibility was, of course, never mentioned.

The district attorney and his wife kept to themselves in a corner of the big cellar. The old gentleman was the last of us to abandon his home. We had already spent five days in the cellar when, in the middle of one terrible night, he made his appearance in a long nightshirt, a nightcap on his head and his flashlight in his hand. His wife followed him, in slippers and muffled up in a thick coat. The district attorney delivered a diatribe against the disrespectful present era. The Russian bullets had whipped right into his bedroom, completely disregarding his wife's Swiss nationality! Next day, the couple definitely settled down among us. The old man had caught cold and taken to his bed with influenza. His wife, with her odd accent and her graying curls, wandered about like a ghost. Citizen of a neutral state, she wore a little Swiss badge, but the armies did not even respect her person! The district attorney and his wife were certainly the most unhappy of us all.

During the first few days, we made each other's acquaintance. We told each other the stories of our lives, sometimes feeling almost glad that this catastrophe had brought us together and given us the chance to exchange confidences. Mr. Radnai was the only exception. Being a Jew, he lived under cover of false papers. The entire apartment house had taken him under its wing to hide him. He was a peaceable man who spent his time reading Heine by the light of his candle.

After a week, people suddenly began hating each other. The banker's widow exclaimed in irritation every time she caught sight of the colonel's lady, and Ilus became hysterical at every coarse remark dropped by the janitor's wife. Faces reflected the inner conflict. The women would have much preferred to hide their alcohol stoves under their pillows rather than let their neighbors know what they were cooking. The men wrangled over the job of getting the water. People circled around each other like angry dogs, each watching for the right moment to tear the other to pieces.

It was during one of these deadly evenings that Pista appeared. He came whistling down the steps and, pushing open the door to the main shelter, said simply, with a broad smile: "Good evening! . . . I wish you good evening. . . ."

He wore the uniform of the Hungarian infantry. A knapsack hung from his shoulder, and his smile was as radiant as if the sun had suddenly lit up our darkness. We formed a circle around him, looking at him as if he had come from another planet. We wanted to touch him to assure ourselves that this was a real human being and not an invention of our tortured imaginations.

He threw his tommy gun on the floor and declared, "Tonight, I'll sleep here. Do you accept me?"

"Who are you?" asked a voice.

"Istvan Nagy. From Pusztaberény, in the county of Somogy."

This introduction sealed our friendship and from then on Pista was one of us. We besieged him with questions: Where were the Russians? How much longer would we have to stay in the cellar? He knew no more than we did. We asked him to which army corps he belonged.

"To none that I know of," he replied calmly. "I move around here and there. Now I'll stay here for a while."

He sat down on a stool, took some bread and bacon from his knapsack, and asked how many of us there were.

"Twelve," answered the banker's widow.

Pista divided his bread and bacon into twelve parts so that everyone could have a bite. We watched him, grateful and amazed. The food melted in our empty mouths like a piously whispered prayer of thanksgiving. Pista had miraculously relaxed the tense atmosphere. But suddenly the district attorney's voice came from a corner of the cellar.

"Deserter!" he gasped from lungs burning with fever. "Can't you see he's a deserter? At a time like this, he ought to be fighting somewhere — if necessary, shedding his blood. . . ."

"What's the matter with the old man?" Pista asked.

"Pneumonia," replied the doctor laconically, as if this were a consultation.

"I'll try to scrounge a bit of sulfa for him tomorrow," promised Pista. "There's still some in a drugstore in the Boulevard Margit. I've gotten it already for several sick people. But right now, I'm going to sleep. I'm tired."

"Are you really going to bring him some medicine?" asked the district attorney's wife, clutching his arm. "Sulfa — that might still save him. . . . Here, take my mattress to stretch out on."

Pista shook his head.

"That's not necessary. The rug's all right for me. Tomorrow I'll bring the medicine and some flour. There's still lots of flour in a store in Express Street. With that you'll have plenty of food."

That night, toward eleven o'clock, a heavy bomber went all out for us. The ground shook and reverberated under our feet. I buried my head in my pillow. But, suddenly, a strange calm came over me.

"Dear God," I whispered, "Thy will be done. . . ."

9

2.

CHAPTER

Pista left at dawn, and while he was away we talked of no one else. The wife of the district attorney anxiously watched for his return because of the medicine; others thrilled at the thought of the flour. Of them all, our family was the worst off for food — just because we had shown too much foresight. By a lucky chance, my parents had been able to rent three rooms in a villa in the Hüvösvölgy, protected by the Swedish flag. From the very beginning of December we had taken all our valuables there as well as quantities of foodstuffs — whole sacks of flour, jars of cooking fat, meat, sugar, coffee, and beverages of all kinds.

We had counted on waiting out the arrival

of the Russians at the villa. But they had taken the area before we got there, and we had to give up all hope of reaching our refuge. In the fall, my father had lent the villa to some friends from Transylvania who had a large family. He had told himself that a small space would be big enough to house a large number of people of good will. The result was that they now had all the food they needed, while we were fasting in our cellar. But nothing could be done about it and, if Pista really did bring us flour, our worries would be over. For we needed bread more than anything. . . .

In the happy expectation of more flour, even the couple who kept a restaurant on the ground floor of the building had joined us. Up to then, these two had kept away, fearing that the tenants might ask for food. They were unwilling to part with it for money and did not yet dare to demand gold in exchange. But now the restaurant keeper's wife was all honey and offered to cook a goulash for lunch. She was even ready to sacrifice a few cans of meat still in her possession. Everyone was to have some of the stew on the strict condition that she got a third of the flour Pista brought back. We all accepted enthusiastically and she returned to her stove. The hours crept by with exasperating slowness, punctuated only by the jerky rhythm of the bombs.

Toward noon, the cellar assumed a holiday

atmosphere. Hearts swelled with joy at the prospect of a good meal. We put a few tables together and covered them with a white cloth; then everyone brought his plate. We waited. Even the district attorney felt better and claimed his share of the goulash. His wife gave the doctor a questioning look: The young man shrugged his shoulders. Nothing could make him any worse ... let him go ahead and eat.

We were all there, sitting around the table as if for a banquet. At last the restaurant-keeping couple appeared, bearing a large casserole. They went all around the table and ladled a big helping of stewed meat onto each plate. We giggled with pleasure. Our doctor bedaubed his face with grease up to the ears, and the banker's widow bent close to her plate as if to drink her goulash instead of eating it. Who thought of death then or of the martyred town crumbling to dust over our heads?

Like so many unchained beasts, we flung ourselves on the pieces of meat; then we leaned back comfortably, staring into space, silently savoring the delight of being replete at last. This meal was memorable for every single one of us. The tenants arranged with the restaurant keeper that, from now on, they would take turns making bread in his oven.

About four o'clock in the afternoon, the house was hit by two bombs. Tiles and pieces of the roof were flung down into the courtyard.

Either our apartment must have been hit or else the district attorney's. It was the front of the building, overlooking the Danube, that had been damaged.

On the twenty-fourth of December in a vain attempt to get to the Hüvösvölgy we had left home so hurriedly that I had left the book I was reading upstairs. It was Balzac's *Peau de Chagrin.* In my mind, I often relived the story I had begun and which I should have liked to finish, but I did not have the courage to go up to the apartment again. The idea of climbing the stairs to the second floor filled me with as much terror as the sight of builders moving about on a narrow plank five floors above the street. In the interval between the two direct hits on the house, I thought of my book, thinking that, even if it were still intact, I should never know how the novel ended because we would — all of us — die here in this cellar.

Sitting on the edge of my bed, I felt my eyes fill with tears at the thought of death. It was not self pity, but an inexplicable sense of loss. Fantastic dreams tormented me at night, and strange adventures, projected in the darkness as on a screen, unrolled before my eyes. I saw myself walking under palm trees on the arm of a young man who never turned his face toward me. I was traveling in an express train and heard the little bell

13

rung by the waiter in the dining car. I went to the theatre and saw the actors speaking words whose sound never reached me. Waking up was always torture: reality, the horrible cellar, the smelly candle and the hollow-eyed shapes wandering about in the half-light. How I longed to take refuge again in the land of dreams! But today's good meal had put me in a better mood, as if the blood flowed faster and warmer in my veins because my hunger was satisfied. And, from now on, there would be bread, lots of good bread.

When he returned toward evening, covered with snow, Pista looked just like Santa Claus. Instead of his knapsack, he had a very heavy sack which he pushed along before him, panting with the effort.

"Weren't you afraid to come such a long way with that big load?" asked Ilus.

Pista smiled.

"I thought the sack would be a protection if a bomb hit me."

The banker's widow sighed.

"At last a fearless man! Just like my poor Albert. . . . Is it pastry flour, my friend, or just ordinary bread flour?"

"One third belongs to me," the restaurant keeper's wife broke in. "I've got a right to it, I've fed everybody here, filled all their bellies."

Pista gave her a searching look. Then he

took a little oblong box out of his pocket and handed it to the district attorney's wife.

"Here's the sulfa."

The woman began to cry as she thanked him.

We surrounded Pista and all stared at the sack of flour as if hypnotized. A sack of life! Pista ordered each of us to bring some receptacle so that he could distribute it fairly.

"The one with the least food may bring the largest container," he called to us.

"You see how fair he is?" I whispered to my mother.

In my eyes, Pista had become a dazzling hero. He was like the Count of Monte Cristo.

The time had come. Pista untied the sack and filled our casserole ahead of the others. A light film of white dust covered the black cement floor. My mother took the casserole and tasted a pinch of flour. Her face took on a different expression.

"It's only plaster," she murmured. "It's only plaster, not flour at all."

She had spoken these words under her breath but everyone heard. The cellar was transformed into an overturned wasps' nest. Using their elbows, everyone pushed to have a taste, and the restaurant keeper's wife screamed: "You gang of cheats! I gave you food because I was expecting flour and now he's brought plaster and I've fed the lot of you. . . ."

Her large face flushed deeper and deeper. Her husband tried vainly to calm her. The woman went toward the door. When she turned to face us, one hand on the latch, I was afraid she had had a stroke, her features were so distorted. But it was only the meanness of her soul that was making her go to pieces before our eyes, while bitter words spurted from her lips.

"The goulash you ate was horse meat, not beef. . . . In Duck Street, there's a dead horse. . . . We cut up its carcass for your meal. Enjoy yourselves now with all that carrion in your bellies. . . ."

She slammed the iron door behind her. Sick at her stomach, Ilus leaned against the wall. . . . For a few minutes, one heard nothing but her efforts not to vomit. In my own stomach, the meal lay as heavy as a stone. At that moment it seemed that nothing worse could happen to us.

"I assure you all this is only silly prejudice," Mr. Radnai suddenly exclaimed from the dark corner that hid him. "Horse meat is no worse than pork or beef — it's just that we aren't used to it. There's no point getting so worked up over it."

My father took up the argument, developing it as if he were in his classroom giving a lecture on Horace.

"Was it not also an erroneous idea to believe

that there would be no fighting in the city and that the war would thus spare the civilian population? Now that the war has invaded our streets, everyone is a soldier, even the sick, the babies, the women, and the old men. So we ought not to get into a panic on the subject of the goulash . . . we may well meet other ordeals which will demand every ounce of our strength."

"The restaurant man's wife is a witch- all the same . . ." said the doctor, ending the debate.

No one contradicted him.

We emptied the disappointing contents of our casserole into the big sack. Suddenly I was seized with such a violent desire to crunch a loaf of good white bread, all hot from the oven, that I felt faint. I returned to our corner and, lying down on the bed, waited for sleep. The ground shook under our feet; machine gun bullets hammered the walls with a hard, dry rattle like a shower of hail. My imagination had almost carried me to the promenade under the palm trees when a sentence reached me through the mists of slumber. It was the voice of my father speaking to my mother: "Pista says they've brought a munitions train along the bank of the Danube, by using the rails of the number 9 streetcar. The last car in the train is opposite our house. We may be blown up at any moment. . . ."

3.

CHAPTER

THE CLOSENESS of the munitions train filled us with terror. Men condemned to death must feel the same way when they hear steps approaching and know it is the executioner.

"One stray bullet could blow us all to pieces," Pista had said. And the bullets were not flying past one at a time but in groups of five or ten. . . .

That morning, the Germans had left three cases of ammunition in the restaurant and brought the horses into the stair well. We watched them from the entrance to the cellar, where we were washing ourselves with dirty snow for lack of anything better. What would become of us without Pista? Knowing that we were living on the edge of a powder magazine was driving us crazy! But having Pista, the soldier, there reassured us. Nothing linked his lot to ours, after all, we told each other; he could go somewhere else if he felt in danger here.

But that did not happen; Pista stayed to keep up our morale. He began by asking each tenant what he would like to have from his apartment and was overwhelmed with requests. I had a new hope that I might now finish my book. During the most violent bombing, Pista ranged through every floor of the building and reported on the state of the premises. He also brought down my Balzac. The blast of the explosions, he told us, had destroyed all the doors in our apartment and that of the district attorney. A dud bomb had demolished our piano by hurtling through it from end to end and was embedded in the parquet floor. This story was, I think, the only pleasure of my entire stay in the cellar. To know that the piano, which had cost me so many hours of forced labor, no longer existed, gave me immense satisfaction. But I did not allow my delight to show, for my mother was crying.

The instrument had been a real friend to her. Accompanying herself, she used to sing charming little French songs whose words I did not understand but which filled me with nostalgia. They made me think, with a mixture of tenderness and desire, of the unknown lover to whom I could one day confide all my troubles and who would take me in his arms to protect me.

The destruction of the piano put an end to one chapter of my adolescent life. Perhaps it was at that moment I realized my childhood had abruptly come to an end, and a fierce pride came over me at the thought that, at fifteen, I should die the death of an adult. Avidly, I began to read my book. I had not read five lines before my eyes began to blur with the effort. But I would not admit that I could hardly see and continued to struggle for each word.

Suddenly a terrifying force lifted me from the couch and flung me against the wall. As I collapsed, half-unconscious, I realized that the skylight, through which a pale light normally filtered, had suddenly darkened. My mouth and eyes filled with dust and, for lack of air, I began to cough. It would have been better to black out completely. I crawled on all fours in the darkness searching for my parents. I found my mother, still conscious, lying in the narrow passage that linked our shelter with the main cellar. As I gently laid my head on her lap, I saw the colonel's wife staggering down the cellar steps, pressing her hands against her mouth. Blood gushed out between her entwined fingers and ran over her arms and dress. My mother sat up and said we must help the injured woman, but we were trembling so much we could not stand.

The victim staggered into the main cellar: we followed her. There, too, it was completely dark and the dust was thick enough to cut. Pista stepped forward and asked for bandages. The injured woman had been in the courtyard at the moment the munitions train had blown up. The blast had hurled her against a wall and had broken her jaw. We did what we could for her, but the blood kept spurting through the layers of absorbent gauze.

In the stair well the panic-stricken horses whinnied frantically. Mr. Radnai, my father, and the doctor went up into the courtyard. Falling fragments of the third floor had killed one of the German soldiers. The courtyard was strewn with rubble and pieces of masonry. Above our heads, the floors were visibly collapsing but we were alive and that was all that mattered.

Pista had gone in search of a doctor. At first, this had offended our doctor, but when he saw that he could not stop the injured woman's hemorrhage, he became silent and went off by himself. The district attorney had improved since the sulfa had lowered his temperature, but he continued to complain about the unheard-of insolence of those responsible for the damage to his home.

"The Swiss flag is displayed over my door," he

cried in a hoarse voice. "It's an extraterritorial residence, protected by a neutral power. . . ."

No one paid any attention to his protests. The banker's wife, kneeling beside her bed, prayed, her jewels clutched in her clasped hands. Ilus' golden hair was covered with soot and her unfortunate baby howled with terror. Even the restaurant keepers tremblingly appeared, although fearing reprisals for the horse-meat stew. We ignored them. Death had brushed us too closely not to wipe out human passions, and we noted in silence the fact that these two had joined us again. The ground floor no longer seemed to offer them any protection since the disappearance of an entire floor over their heads. Had the explosion burst their eardrums? They no longer seemed to hear. The colonel's wife was stretched out on her bed, still bleeding. The bulky, energetic woman watched us with incredulous eyes, as if she could not understand why fate had struck her down.

At last Pista returned with a doctor. He told us with horror that the big apartment house in the Vitéz-utca had been reduced to a heap of rubble and that the tenants would be asphyxiated if the safety exit could not be cleared quickly. From all the neighboring houses men were leaving the cellars to lend their aid and our men also went to help under Pista's escort.

A strange calm flooded our hearts. The mu-

nitions train had blown up and we were alive.
. . . But I bit my fingers to stifle the cry of terror
that rose to my lips at the thought that we, we
too, might have suffered the fate of those who
were buried alive.

All afternoon I struggled against the vision of
faces convulsed by suffocation. I imagined that
we were trapped under the debris and that
every breath we took consumed a little of the
life left to us. These hallucinations did not
leave me an instant's peace. I had to talk about
them to someone so I went into the big cellar
and sat down beside Mr. Radnai. He closed his
book and looked at me.

"What's the matter?" he asked. "Are you
ill? Come, let's go up for a moment," he suggested, and put the book into his pocket.

We passed close by the bed where the colonel's wife lay, moaning in her fever; the doctor
sat quietly beside her.

We went up to see the horses tethered in
the stair well and I noticed with horror that
one of them was nibbling the banisters, and
had already swallowed a morsel of wood. A
bloody saliva drooled from its cracked lips and
dribbled over its chest.

"Not one bullet to put these poor beasts
out of their misery," said Mr. Radnai, as if
he were swearing. "An ammunition train blows
up just beside us, the restaurant is packed
with high explosives; the steel of the cannons

is melting, they're firing so much to use up the shells before the Russians arrive, and these wretched animals will perish of hunger and thirst!"

The horses surrounded us, whinnying their complaint, staring at us with bulging, bloodshot eyes. I could not endure their look and hung my head. One of the horses came up and gently nudged my back, as if urging me to take pity and bring them at least a little food and water. An intense, crushing despair seized hold of me. I put my arm around the horse's neck and burst into tears.

Mr. Radnai took my hand and drew me back toward the entrance to the cellar. Gently he stroked my hair.

"Poor little girl! Poor generation! . . . How pitiful!"

I stopped at the first step.

"No, I can't go back to the cellar," I told Mr. Radnai. "It will collapse and bury us."

"Don't be afraid . . . nothing more will happen now. Go on down. . . ."

"Aren't you frightened?" I asked point blank.

"But of course I'm frightened! I'm afraid of suffocating to death. I've no idea what has happened to my family, and my life depends on the whim of a few hysterical people. When will they denounce me . . . or betray my Jewish origin by a careless word?"

"Don't be afraid of that," I told him. "No one would dream of harming you."

We went down in silence. Mr. Radnai took his place again and brought out his little suede-bound book. But I noticed that, instead of reading, he stared fixedly into space.

About six o'clock the men returned without having discovered the safety exit of the collapsed building. A young man and young woman were with them. The girl, about twenty-two or twenty-three, clutched her fur-lined coat about her, shivering, and never for a moment let go the boy's hand. We watched them without saying a word. Who were they and what did they want of us?

It was Pista who spoke: "They come from the Vitéz-utca. They had gone to fetch water when the munitions train blew up and they're the only survivors. . . . They must stay here for, after all, they can't wander about the streets. I hope you will take them in . . . I'll manage to find food for them somehow. . . ."

We stared at them, petrified, as if they were ghosts. They did not seem to belong to the real world. Like St. Thomas, we would have liked to touch them, to feel them, to make sure they were truly alive.

Ilus, who was holding her baby on her arm, was the first to speak. She went up to them.

"Dear God," she said, "I can see that these two love each other. . . . How young they are . . .

even death has had pity on them. . . . What can I do to help? If there is anything whole in my apartment, you may bring down whatever you wish. And I'll also share my food with you."

The banker's wife promised them cooking utensils, the restaurant keeper's wife offered a can of meat, the medical student asked if they were hurt anywhere.

A charitable feeling toward them rose in every heart, as if this were the moment to settle forever the debt of gratitude we owed to fate. Pista and the doctor brought down a large couch and some blankets from Ilus' apartment. Then they went off in search of some food from the big grocery in the Fo-utca. It was the first time the doctor had risked leaving the cellar. The banker's widow called out from her corner: "You might also bring a little meat for a stew."

The restaurant keeper's wife went white . . . this was a "stone in her garden." But the old lady went on: "The horse is an animal, just as the pig is. The only thing that matters is the meat must be fresh. Personally, I'm not disgusted by it any more. . . . I'm hungry."

The others said nothing, but these words were received by the two restaurant owners like an absolution. Ilus moved into our cellar, leaving her coal bin to the young couple, Eve and Gabriel. . . .

We no longer questioned their presence.

It seemed as natural for them to be here as if they had lived with us for years. The thing that really mattered to me now was the *Peau de Chagrin*. Trying frantically to read, I came too close to the sticky candle wick and my hair burst into flames. I screamed. My mother flung a blanket over my head, but nothing was left of my curls which, until then, had hung down to my shoulders. My neck, too, was painfully burned. They put ointment on my ear and Pista, armed with an enormous pair of scissors, cut off the last uneven locks of my hair. It was a melancholy boy who stared back at me from the tarnished mirror I still possessed. I no longer recognized myself.

The days dragged by: fearful nightmares and battles against a world of phantoms. My dream country had vanished. Sleep no longer led me toward peace, but toward lunar landscapes of evil and horror.

Pista often disappeared for whole days but always returned smiling, like someone over whom even death had no dominion.

After one particular night, we waited, exhausted, for the dawn. The explosions had followed one another in an unbroken rhythm. Every time the house suffered a direct hit, the ground under our feet shuddered as if the earth, too, were inhabited by infernal powers.

At half-past six, Pista woke everyone up. He

told us that the Germans had, that very night, blown up all the bridges over the Danube.

We could not take in this stupefying news. Unbelieving, we stared at the speaker; then, on a common impulse, we decided to verify his words with our own eyes. We filed up the great staircase in a strange procession, the thought never occurring to us that a bomb, falling without warning, might blow us to pieces. The destruction of the bridges had eclipsed all other fears . . . yet this indifference itself was perhaps the most frightening thing of all. We gathered in the colonel's apartment. Pista forbade us to show ourselves, saying that on the other side of the river Russian sharpshooters were aiming at every human silhouette. Huddled against the walls, we peered through the ruined windows. The disemboweled bridges lay like fallen trees in the troubled waters of the Danube.

Horrified, I studied the shattered Lanc-hid (the Chain Bridge), thinking of the countless times I had crossed it with my father. I had often met him at the Lanc-hid Café and afterwards we had gone for a walk. Dear old Lanc-hid, what have they done to you? And, over there in the distance, was the Elizabeth Bridge, also completely destroyed. It was swathed in the morning mists, as if hiding its huge, shattered body. In my mind I saw once again its light, graceful arch that linked Pest to Buda in a single span like a musical phrase, like a streamer flung over the rushing water by a playful hand.

The powerful river that used to carry pretty pleasure boats seemed to be bruised by contact with the twisted ironwork; it seethed into giddy whirlpools and, in its impotent rage, hurled great blocks of ice against the quays on either bank.

A bomb quite close to us shook us out of our stupor and we returned to the cellar. I lingered behind and threw one last look at the bridges which lay prone before me, like great, unburied corpses.

In the afternoon we vainly sought for water. Everyone returned with empty pails. The faucet in the Kacsa-utca no longer yielded a single drop. . . .

I was thirsty.

4.

CHAPTER

FOR TWO DAYS we had not had a drop of water. Ilus used the last half-glassful to make some warm gruel for the baby with the remainder of the dried milk. The poor child was so weak he could not sit up; he lay there, day after endless day, flaccid, his head lolling, plaintive wails stifled in his throat.

About noon, someone suddenly cried out. I ran to see what had happened. It was the banker's widow, dressed only in her underwear, who was making the commotion.

"Look, I've found a louse!" she pointed. "It's really the last straw that we can't even wash ourselves any more!" And she displayed a sleepy louse on a scrap of old newspaper to anyone who cared to look. We gathered round and stared at the insect. The event was so portentous that, for a few moments, we forgot our thirst.

Outside, hell had broken loose once again. Since morning, the house had been hit seven times and we never stopped praising God for the solid vaulted cellars of the hundred-year-old building; what would have become of us in a modern house with cardboard walls? Even where we were, at a depth equal to the height of a whole floor, the ground never stopped trembling under our feet, as if an electric cable ran beneath the entire city of Budapest, and we continually walked on high-tension wires.

I got in the habit of sitting on the edge of my bed with my legs tucked under me. Every time I put my feet down, I shuddered, I was so terrified by the incessant trembling.

When the water gave out, the janitor and his wife disappeared. They had accumulated stores of food and several people claimed to have seen them carrying a small cask down to the cellar, which, from its appearance, must have contained wine. They stayed hidden in their private cellar in order not to share their treasures with anyone.

That afternoon, however, we saw the janitor when he staggered off to empty the sanitary pail in the courtyard. He seemed even paler and more shrunken than usual and walked past with bent head and such an unsteady gait that twice he allowed his pail to slop over. No one, however, dared make the slightest objection. Everyone knew that the janitor was a Communist and the tenants were afraid that some remark might make him take revenge on us when the Russians entered the town.

About four o'clock in the afternoon, there was an unexpected silence. The Germans, dragging with them a little gun mounted on an armored car, had left their post in front of the house. The street suddenly became calm and deserted.

Slowly, we climbed into the courtyard. The horses had already gnawed the railing of the great staircase as far as the first floor. One of them had grown so feeble that it could only squat on its hindquarters. It was the first time in my life that I had seen a horse sitting down. He, also, would have liked to approach the banisters to satisfy his hunger but he lacked the strength to do so and the other horses were eating his portion.

Then Pista burst in, unexpectedly as usual, but this time empty-handed. We promptly gathered round him to ask advice about the lack of water. He told us our only chance of finding some was at the Turkish baths, not far away, for they were not connected with the city water supply.

Although the baths were only ten minutes away, the distance suddenly seemed to us insuperable. The idea of leaving the shelter of the cellar to cross a street where, at any moment, a shell or bomb might blow us to pieces was unthinkable. Pista was ready to go, but what good would two pailsful be among twenty thirsty, dirty people?

"Personally, I'm going," announced the banker's widow, "and, if there's the slightest possibility, I shall take a bath at once. It's really too much to become verminous at this stage."

These suggestions were followed by a discussion, which seemed endless, about who was to take part in the expedition. Finally, it was decided that everyone should go, with the exception of two who were appointed to keep guard over the cellar. We set off, armed with our pails, but, once in the street, we instinctively began to run.

"Keep calm!" shouted Pista, to quiet our fears. "Running won't help you dodge the shells!"

Those who were keeping watch from the porches of other houses plucked up courage on seeing us outdoors. Our little bucket brigade soon swelled to the size of a procession.

We reached the former baths at a run. A blast had torn the main door off its hinges: to enter, we had to climb over a large stone that blocked the entrance. Inside, on the mosaic floor, lay the corpses of two horses, their legs sticking in the air, their stomachs swollen as if filled with water to the bursting point. We walked round them cautiously and slipped through the opening (once a swinging door) that led to the gallery alongside the sunken baths. In peacetime this part, adorned with palms and tropical plants in stone urns, was the place where white-clad bath attendants received their clients in an atmosphere of hot steam. If Pista had not been with us, we should certainly have gone astray in the icy, deserted labyrinth. It was a question now of finding the main hydrant which fed the baths with boiling, sulphurous water.

"We'll be there in a moment," said Pista, taking the lead. We followed him but suddenly, as if paralyzed with dismay, the entire group stopped short. Not understanding what might have happened, I stepped forward to find out. It was then that my eyes fell on the corpse at the end of the bath. He was floating, with glassy eyes and open mouth, on the surface of the gray-green water. The dampness had so mildewed his clothes that it was impossible to tell whether he was a Hungarian or a German, a soldier or a civilian — a brilliant example of the broad justice dealt by death that makes no distinction between moral principles or nationalities.

Above our heads, the roof had collapsed and we could see the sky; beams and tiles were heaped on both sides of the sunken bath and this pile of ruins presented an insurmountable obstacle.

"We can't possibly reach the water," wailed someone in the crowd, and Ilus burst into hysterical sobs.

"Wait a second," said Pista, disappearing among the rubbish.

He reappeared shortly, straining with the effort of dragging a long plank behind him. After placing it from one end to the other of the bath, he ran across it.

"You can come over," he called. "It easily holds one person at a time."

The melancholy procession moved forward in gloomy silence. What a sad picture we presented, unhappy cityfolk torn from peaceful everyday lives, advancing uncertainly, across the narrow, slippery plank while, at the end of the bath, the dead man staring skywards with great, startled eyes seemed to count steps as he watched the staggering progress.

The first across looked back at us from the far side as the Blessed look back at souls waiting in purgatory. A false step and one would fall beside the drowned man.

It came my turn to cross. My whole body was trembling. They told me to wait for the return of the others, but the thought of being left alone with the dead man filled me with horror. Had my mother also stayed behind, we should not have had enough water and who knew when we might have another chance to come again? I put one foot on the plank and it seemed to me that I was having to walk a tightrope above an immense precipice in the mountains. I had gone nearly halfway when the plank swayed. I screamed and fell on my knees, only to find myself face to face with the dead man. Pista joined me in two bounds, seized me in his arms and deposited me on the other side.

A wild desire made me forget everything, for there before me were the water faucets. The pipes were so badly damaged that the hot, sulphurous water was escaping everywhere, roaring like a waterfall. Nevertheless, we had to give up the idea of drinking it, for the first mouthful had been enough to burn our lips. The banker's widow stripped off her blouse and ran under a shower that, by some miracle, was still functioning.

"You'll scald yourself," shrieked my mother.

"It's cold," the other shouted in return.

We all rushed forward to enjoy the cold water of the shower. Nearly everyone had undressed. It was a voluptuous delight to bare our filthy skins, itching with perspiration, to the stream of water. A piece of soap went the rounds and grateful looks were directed at Ilus, who had brought it and was gladly sharing it. All modesty had vanished; the colonel's wife, naked to the waist, was busy washing her slip and Ilus tucked up her skirt to her thighs and rubbed her feet and legs.

Our joy suddenly changed to terror when a mine exploded close by. We dressed quickly and started back with brimming pails. Despite the bombs which fell thicker and faster than ever, Pista nimbly ran to and fro on the plank to help the weaker ones with their pails. Once in the street, we ran close to the walls, slopping precious liquid on the ground as we went.

In front of the house, the little cannon was already barking away. . . . What joy when, at last, we crossed the threshold of the street door, safe and sound! We seemed to forget that it took only a single bomb to bring the whole building down on us; we only cherished the thought that these old walls would surely protect us from machine gun bullets and bursting mines.

As I crossed the courtyard to the cellar, a feeling stronger than myself pulled me toward the horses. My pails were still half-full. Never in my life shall I forget that moment, even if I live to be very old. I first went up to the sitting horse and offered him water. His happy whinnying reminded me of our cries of joy on reaching the baths. He shivered and inhaled it in great, endless gulps. Slowly, uncertainly, the other horses came forward. I had to continue the distribution very carefully so that each one should have his share. In the eyes of the animals there was an almost human expression of gratitude. The horses surrounded me, weak as they were; blood flowed from their gums and suppurating tears from their eyes.

As I returned with my empty pails to the cellar, I felt my heart light and overflowing with joy as if, in the serene days of peace, someone had given me a magnificent present.

5.

LITTLE BY LITTLE, we got in the habit of running to Pista whenever we needed anything and usually he succeeded in filling all our most urgent requests.

One morning we asked him to bring, from the convent about a half hour's walk away, a priest who could say the Mass. By now Pista seemed to us completely invulnerable; capable of warding off falling mines and bombs with a wave of his hand, as if he carried a talisman.

Our hope was fulfilled far sooner than we had expected. Barely two days passed before Pista announced that Mass would be said in the cellar on the following morning. (It was truly strange to hear those words "morning," "afternoon," or "evening" pronounced in the cellar's perpetual darkness; our eyes, permanently red and watering from the feeble yellow light of the cooking-fat candles, could not measure the hours or the days.) The only fixed point in our timetable was the night bomber who ended his work of destruction about four in the morning; after that, comparative silence reigned until about six.

The great day arrived. Everyone was up and stirring by half-past three in the morning. It had snowed during the night and we were able to wash a little in the snow from the courtyard. In the middle cellar, a table was set and covered with the last clean cloth we had; we noticed with astonishment that even Mr. Radnai had shaved and put on a tie. The banker's widow carefully removed the curlers from her hair, and Ilus put a clean shirt on the baby. The day before, Pista had stolen some candles from a shop — six of them as thick as one's arm. These were a priceless treasure.

A few minutes after four, the old priest arrived, bringing the Blessed Sacrament in a golden pyx and the altar wine in a flask. We had transformed a corner of Ilus' cellar into a confessional, with a chair for the confessor and a blanket on the ground for the penitents. Then we stood in line and the confessions began.

With bowed head, avoiding all glances, Mr. Radnai lined up with the others. The janitor and his wife were there, dressed as if they were going to High Mass in their own village. Eve clung to Gabriel's hand; they stood a little apart. The district attorney had a temperature of 105°; he was delirious and would receive the Last Sacrament. The candles were lit on the improvised altar and the cellar was suddenly flooded with golden light. Shadows with bowed heads passed me to kneel before the altar. Pista smoothed out the last wrinkles in the cloth; then he, too, took his place in line.

When my turn came, I felt my heart thumping violently.

"I don't want to die, Father," I told him almost in tears. "I am only fifteen and I am horribly afraid of death. I want to go on living."

The pale face with the lowered eyelids remained motionless in front of me. How often must he have heard the same rebellious words, how often must someone have clutched his hand, saying: "Father, life still owes me so much. One cannot perish in this darkness and filth when there are countries where the sun is shining, where people are walking about in the streets while we are besieged here in this city that has become a graveyard."

I heard myself say: "Father, I'm terrified every time I go out, because I cannot help stepping on the dead. Their glassy eyes accuse me because I am still among the living. . . ."

"The fate of our bodies matters very little," the priest answered gently. "The death we fear so much is only a deliverance: the moment when the soul escapes from its bodily prison to enter into eternity. And God loves us so much, my child! He welcomes us with infinite love. In His kingdom there are no wars — no death, either. Sunshine, peace, and sublime joy wait for us there. Can we fear such things? As to the dead who surround us here, don't imagine they accuse us; on the contrary, they pity us for having to endure the sufferings of this life. Do not forget that none of those who have died here among the ruins is lost for eternal life. . . ."

As I came away, I was no longer aware of anyone about me. Through the warm mist of my tears, the light of the candles reflected all the colors of the rainbow; the walls had vanished to give place to a magnificent cathedral in which the light seemed to grow more and more radiant as if a golden flood of sunbeams had come in. Trembling voices were singing hymns and a feeling of pure joy swept me to the verge of ecstasy.

It was a long time before I returned to reality and saw Eve and Gabriel kneeling in front of the altar. The priest was solemnizing their marriage. It was unforgettable, that vow of faithfulness unto death, pronounced here on the brink of eternity and in the perpetual shadow of death.

The priest left about seven that morning,

when the bombardment was at its height. It looked as if this day would be even more terrible than the ones before. The house had already been severely damaged and part of the third floor hall had been hurled into the courtyard.

Everyone looked for some small present for the young couple. Mr. Radnai offered them an orange. He had hoarded this fruit, already completely dried up, for more than five weeks, saving it for still harder times. The janitor brought a glass of wine. Everyone celebrated their happiness.

Later, Eve sought out Ilus in her little cellar to give her the orange for the baby.

6.

CHAPTER

THAT AFTERNOON was terrible. I sat on the edge of my bed without daring to put my feet down, I hated the continual shuddering so much. The cooking-fat candle wavered as it shed its yellow light. I longed to read but my eyes watered after a few minutes. My mother never stopped warning me that later I should have to wear glasses.

What did I care about the state of my eyes, when, as I thought then, I had only a few days to live? At that moment, I was no longer afraid of death; only the passage from this life to eternal life worried me. Should we all be killed when the bombs brought the house down over our heads? Would we suffocate under the ruins or would we be burned alive by the flame throwers? If the Germans made us leave the house, we should become magnificent targets for the Russians posted on the opposite bank. They would shoot us down one after the other with their telescopic rifles; they would even be able to enjoy our grimaces before seeing us collapse in death.

Pista decided to steal a wedding veil for Eve. He claimed to remember a nearby dress shop where one could buy them before the siege. In the window, instead of little hats with feathers, there was now an unexploded bomb. But Pista was sure he would find a veil inside. We tried to dissuade him, but he laughed and his splendid, healthy white teeth shone in the candlelight.

"I want this to be an unforgettable day for Eve," he kept saying.

He did not go alone, for the doctor wanted to go with him. Hunger had reached such a point in our household that the latter's decision was received almost with joy. The doctor was expert at dissection; outside he would surely find the carcass of a horse from which to cut the best portions so the restaurant keeper's wife could make us a nourishing soup and a meat dish.

Our horses were still alive. Those of us who lived directly under the main staircase were aware of them all the time, for they kept pawing the ground with their hooves. Pista told us that the horse who could not stand was so weak now that it lay stretched out and had strength enough to lift its head only when anyone came near. I was impatiently waiting for the next opportunity to bring water for them to drink.

"It's seven o'clock," said Mr. Radnai, who had come to chat with my father. "Pista still hasn't returned."

We grew more and more uneasy. Ilus, especially, was desperately anxious for, if the young man did not return, the baby would have nothing to eat the next day; the last can of dried milk was empty.

"A quarter to eight," said Mr. Radnai some time later, scratching his chin. "Odd, the little mechanism of this watch," he went on, thinking aloud. "It was manufactured in Switzerland . . . I can hardly believe that country still exists . . . Switzerland . . . glaciers, pure air, winter sports, luxury hotels full of tourists, an obsequious headwaiter asking if one would prefer lobster or crayfish . . ."

The smell of cooking was wafted through the cellars. Good heavens! Smell of cooking, what a marvelous, mouth-watering expression. . . . Oh, we must eat! Eat? No, engulf! Devour!

"No doubt you have traveled a great deal, Professor?"

"Yes," replied my father. Then he gripped my arm, for I had just cried out with terror: An explosion, very near indeed, had shaken us all. The door of our cellar shot open, as if impelled by the blast of a bomb, but it was the janitor. He was livid and his trembling lips could scarcely articulate: "Come at once . . . they've brought him back . . ."

"Pista?" I gasped. A terrible presentiment tightened my throat.

We rushed into the passage, jostling one another. The doctor unloaded Pista from his shoulders. Both were as covered with blood as if they had been dipped in red paint.

"Is he unconscious?" asked a hoarse voice from the rear.

"He's quite dead," replied the doctor timidly, almost apologetically. "We had gone a long way when a mine exploded right in front of him. The blast flung me against a wall. When the dust and smoke cleared, I saw he was dead."

The banker's widow was seized with nausea and stumbled out of the passage. The sweetish smell of blood penetrated into our very brains. Ilus burst into sobs.

"Here's his sack," continued the doctor. "It holds the things that were meant for you."

He handed the sack to Ilus who took it with trembling fingers. She fumbled interminably untying the string, but no one helped her for we were all chilled with horror. Bending over her task, she was smeared with blood to her elbows before at last she managed to open the sack. Her shaking hands drew out three cans of condensed milk. She burst into a shrill laugh.

"Milk for my baby . . . he won't die of hunger! Dear God, it's milk for my baby! For my poor little baby, lovely milk for my baby."

It was some time before she could pull herself together. Then, fumbling in the bottom of the sack, she drew out a beautiful white veil.

"The wedding veil," said Mr. Radnai in a toneless voice, as the little cannon at the corner of the street began to bark. Eve hid her face in her hands and obstinately shook her head.

"I don't want it — don't give it to me."

Then Ilus, holding the veil, approached what had once been Pista and covered him with the filmy, white fabric. Her gesture was gentle and motherly, as if she were covering her sleeping child.

"Thank you," she whispered over and over. "Thank you. . . ."

The narrow passage was transformed into a mortuary chapel. We all knelt and Eve said a prayer aloud. The veil slowly became saturated with blood; outside, the shrapnel spattered in bursts.

That night the bombs followed one another without a break.

At midday we had drunk the remaining water. Now there was no more water, not a drop of water — only blood, blood, everywhere blood.

7.
CHAPTER

THE NEWS spread that, at dawn, the Russians had occupied the barracks in the neighboring street, a building in which about ten Germans had been besieged for more than two weeks. Our liberation could hardly be delayed much longer. Once the Russians entered the city, we should be able to return to the upper floors and stop living like rats in the cellar.

It must have been nearly seven o'clock when four Germans, heavily armed, erupted noisily into the courtyard. They laid down their tommy guns and labored, with great difficulty, to mount a bazooka on the staircase. Then, loaded with heavy cases of ammunition, they moved into the few rooms on the first floor that were still more or less intact.

These maneuvers puzzled us. It looked as if they intended to transform the building into a fortress and defend it to the bitter end.

Now it seemed impossible that we should escape being killed for, once the house was besieged, the flame throwers must roast us alive.

With hardly a breath of strength left in him, so weakened was he by fever, the district attorney raised himself in his bed, gasping hoarsely: "Insolent dogs! They want to shoot from my apartment! My wife's a Swiss, I shall complain to the minister."

His white beard flowed over his sweat-soaked nightshirt. Waving his bony arms, he looked like a skeleton in the blinking light of the candles. Over the raucous sobs of the janitor's wife, which nearly deafened us, Mr. Radnai tried to make himself heard, although speaking in a low voice: "Look here, keep calm! As soon as the Russians appear, I'll put on my yellow star so that they'll know that I'm a Jew. Then I'll be able to protect you as you're protecting me now by hiding me from the Germans."

The banker's wife retorted anxiously: "Do you plan to stand up against fighting troops with a star? Do you think that will be the slightest use?"

"Why of course. The star is a symbol; it's the emblem of the persecuted. From now on it will be the sign of the apotheosis of the martyrs."

Ilus had come in, carrying the child wrapped

in a blanket. An inexpressible feeling drove us together; it was frightening to be alone.

My father, who had stayed sitting in a corner, absorbed in his thoughts, exclaimed suddenly: "Look! Is that water dripping from the wall?"

We clustered around him and saw that glittering drops beaded the saltpeter-covered wall.

"Can we drink it?" asked someone in a faltering voice. "We should catch it in something."

No one answered; we stared at the wall, fascinated. The flow increased; we saw, with horror, a very thin but ever-increasing stream of water spreading over the floor. It was flooding into the cellar from all sides.

"We must bail it out at once," said the doctor sharply. "We'll form a chain with buckets and empty them outside, passing them along from one to the other. But quickly! Otherwise we'll be drowned!"

"Turn off the faucet!" shouted the district attorney. "Or call the plumber. . . . This is too much!"

Out of breath, he fell back on his pillows. We ran to get pails and Ilus settled her whimpering baby in the bed beside the lawyer so that she, too, might help in the task.

We formed a line from the cellar to the street and passed pails from hand to hand as quickly as possible. The last man in the line emptied them into the street.

The Germans came down and stood watching us at work.

"You're giving yourselves trouble for nothing," said one of them. "The wrecked bridges and the piled-up blocks of ice have dammed the flow of the Danube, and water's rising in the sewers as it does in a canal lock. You don't imagine you're going to keep the Danube out of your cellar with a few pails?"

We stared at him without wishing to understand and our hands went on mechanically passing buckets filled to the brim.

Meanwhile, the little cannon in front of the house began to fire again, which showed that the Russian fighter planes would soon be coming.

Those who were working in the most exposed area were frequently relieved, for only the cellar and the stairs offered any shelter. We kept at our job relentlessly for five hours, threatened always by volleys of machine gun fire and exploding mines. We had no choice between this dangerous work, which could produce no satisfactory result, and the prospect of being drowned by the stinking water rising in the cellar.

At noon, word reached us that the water was receding; doubtless it had found another outlet and danger was momentarily averted.

Worn-out, drenched with sweat, and, above all, terribly hungry, we went back to the cellar, so long our only shelter and now ice-cold and horrible.

The sewer smell impregnated the blankets, the few bits of furniture, and the flour we had kept for an occasional treat and which we ate in little pinches from time to time.

We forced ourselves to act as if nothing had happened. The danger of flooding had passed; the cellar still protected us from the firing that made the upper floors uninhabitable. But fear gripped our throats. The janitor's wife wept continuously and her hoarse voice was like the grating of a saw.

Early in the afternoon, the door of the cellar suddenly opened and a German appeared with a tommy gun in his fist.

"*Raus!*" he shouted. "Go up at once into the courtyard, all of you!"

We assailed him with questions. What had happened? Why must we leave the cellar?

But he only said he pitied anyone who stayed behind. The district attorney's wife thrust herself forward.

"I'm quite willing to go up myself, but my husband is very ill with pneumonia and he's an old man of eighty. At least, leave him in peace."

"Everyone must go," insisted the German. "I wouldn't care to be in the skin of anyone the commanding officer finds here!"

We had to obey. The district attorney was

helped, not to say carried, by his wife and the doctor. Mr. Radnai turned up his coat collar and walked with his head bowed. The banker's widow hastily put on some lipstick. Eve and Gabriel walked arm-in-arm, radiant with a happiness that neither life nor death could touch.

The German kicked open the janitor's door; the woman did not even raise her eyes. After the third summons, he seized her by the arm and dragged her into the courtyard.

When we were all gathered together, we waited in silence. The doctor looked uneasy. Four Germans armed with tommy guns confronted us. Their commanding officer announced: "Our rations have been stolen. Two men will search the cellar."

The soldiers he indicated went below. Several people tried to speak and the district attorney declared indignantly that an accusation of theft was an insult. But the officer interrupted in a harsh voice.

"Silence!"

After a quarter of an hour, the two Germans reappeared and announced that they had found nothing. After consulting his watch, their commander said: "Listen, everybody: The ground floor is filled with munitions. If, in five minutes, you do not return our rations, I shall blow up the building. I don't have to account to anyone for this act, for I shan't leave Budapest alive. And if the ruins of this house block the street, the Russians will have that much more difficulty in getting through. I am counting the five minutes!"

I felt my body go numb. It became as cold and alien as if I were already dead.

The doctor burst into sobs. This man who dissected dead horses with the utmost detachment was weeping with emotion and terror.

"I've not stolen anything," he moaned. "Let me go!"

Ilus, exhausted from holding the child so long in her arms, slipped gently to the ground. Squatting on the dirty snow, she breathed on the baby's face to soften the rigor of the cold.

"Four minutes to go," said the German.

The janitor's wife, who had been one of the fattest women in the capital and who, after the death of her son some weeks before, had become so emaciated as to be unrecognizable, stared at us like someone counting the number of condemned men on a scaffold. Her sorrow was a little appeased. So far, she had nourished a bitter hatred against the living, but now that we all had only a few moments to live, rancor had left her.

Abruptly, the banker's widow tore off the little bag of jewels hanging from her neck and, stepping forward, offered it to the Germans.

"Let me go and this fortune is yours."

The soldiers remained perfectly still, not showing the slightest interest. One might have thought we were no longer dealing with men of flesh and blood but with robots.

My father and mother were holding my hands, gripping my fingers more and more tightly.

The district attorney screamed that he wanted to live. I told myself that he had already lived eighty years while *I* was only fifteen and had more reason to weep than he. . . .

The great walls of the house seemed to sway. I could see nothing but the blurred outlines of the German soldiers in front of me. Only the fierce pressure of my father's and mother's hands kept me alive in the midst of this courtyard filled with ruins. Then I heard some words in German, and I felt myself falling to the bottom of a dark abyss.

On regaining consciousness, I found myself once more in the cellar which I both hated and loved so much, and I dissolved in tears. People gathered around, making a fuss over me. Sobs convulsed me like an electric current. They explained that, before the five minutes of grace were up, a Hungarian soldier had shouted from one of the windows on the second floor that he would return the German army rations if the civilians were left in peace.

He must have been a soldier of the disbanded troops, like Pista. No one ever knew what became of him after his confession.

8.

CHAPTER

NIGHT FELL and those who had been up in the courtyard announced that the banks of the Danube were lit up with red flares. In this way the Russians were designating the places they would encircle with artillery fire. This news aroused no one. We were too exhausted. The episode of that afternoon had sapped the last of our strength.

By eight o'clock, the battle was raging. The house was constantly shaken by shells and the bombers, whose droning we heard continuously, were attacking the quarter in waves.

At ten o'clock, the flooding began again. We watched the level rise from one minute to the next. Impossible for our pails to keep up with it, flight was the only solution. But where could we go? Where could we find a shelter that offered any safety? We had no time for thought; the water was already up to our knees. Everyone hurriedly gathered up the necessities. We stuffed our pockets with the few remaining handfuls of dried beans and rescued the blankets which we had to hold high to keep them above the water. Mr. Radnai dressed himself hastily with the water reaching up to his shirttails. Ilus wrapped up her baby. The banker's widow shrieked and gesticulated wildly. Eve and Gabriel helped all of us, for they had nothing of their own to save.

We loaded our pitiful belongings on our shoulders and set out toward the staircase through water which now came up to our waists. The district attorney rode pickaback on Mr. Radnai's shoulders, and each of us clutched a precious grease candle.

A German tried to force us back into the cellar, but, when he shone his flashlight on the foot of the staircase, he saw the black waves storming the steps. He showed us a door on the ground floor, saying that anyone who dared to leave by that exit would get a bullet through his body.

We found ourselves in the janitor's apartment. The district attorney and the baby were tucked up in the bed.

With the first light of dawn a complete silence fell as if by magic. We dared not believe our ears and listened with our heads to the wall.

The doctor declared he was going to see what was happening outside. Everyone protested, for even to push the door ajar would have been enough to invite a volley of machine-gun fire. But he shrugged his shoulders.

"Death's inevitable now and I'd rather fall by a bullet than be burned alive."

He moved to the door, turned the handle, and crossed the threshold. Trembling all over, I stuffed my fingers into my ears but did not hear the shots I was expecting with such terror. A few moments later, the doctor's voice rang out through the silence.

"Hey! You can come out now. They've gone. Everyone's left the house!"

Frantic with joy, we shouted and yelled. The district attorney hopped about on one leg, shrieking at the top of his voice:

"The Germans have gone! We're saved!"

It was the eighty-year-old man who rejoiced the most at this slim hope of life.

Mr. Radnai's lips were still blue with fear, but already he was saying confidently: "I was sure they would go. You know, I have presentiments about such things."

But no one paid attention.

We staggered into the courtyard. It was beginning to be light; somewhere in the east the sun was climbing the edge of the horizon to bathe the ruined city of Budapest in its rays.

The courtyard was full of machine guns and arms of various kinds and littered with ammunition and empty cartridge cases. In front of the porte-cochere lay a German soldier's cap. Two cases of unused shells yawned open beside the deserted A.A. gun.

In this strange, smoky atmosphere things no longer had any reality: the courtyard, the street, the whole city, blurred in a ghastly light, looked like a landscape on the moon. Abandoned weapons lay everywhere. Opposite us, a house had collapsed on its inmates whom death had surprised in the middle of their horrible fight against suffocation. There, on the right, was the fragment of a fourth floor apartment where a piano hung supported only by a few bricks; of the room next door, which must have been a bathroom, nothing remained but a wall with a towel rack.

Everywhere, as far as we could see, were ruins, ruins, and more ruins.

In front of the candy shop on the corner lay the bodies of the three horses we had led from our stair well. The sweetish, penetrating odor of decay surrounded us. We did not know then that the air of the town would be permeated with this loathsome smell for many long weeks to come.

But where had the Germans gone? It seemed as if they had evacuated the street. But that was impossible. Why this silence? Fear overwhelmed us. The silence became heavier and heavier. The banker's widow guessed that the Russians must already have arrived, for they had held the neighboring district for the past three months. But where were they?

The uncertainty was appalling! We had the feeling we were being watched from behind the walls, the ruins, even the corpses of the horses. The Russians must be very close, perhaps in the next building. Or did they think the Germans were still in our house and were they preparing a fresh assault?

Panic made us retreat, first to the porch and then to rooms on the ground floor.

After an anxious, fifteen-minute wait, Ilus ran in, out of breath, and said that a wounded German had just been discovered under the stairs. We all hurried to the scene. There, behind the great marble staircase, where once baby carriages had been stored, a young soldier lay in a pool of blood.

"It only needed this," exclaimed Mr. Radnai. "If the Russians find him here, we shall all be executed."

In a few moments, we were all gathered around the wounded man, who was losing quantities of blood.

"We must look after him," suggested Ilus in

a hesitating voice. "I'll bring some cloth for a bandage."

"Don't be in such a hurry," replied Mr. Radnai. "This man would have had no scruples about letting us die in our cellar. And, if the Russians learn that we've given aid to a German, heaven help us!"

The district attorney had arrived, leaning on his wife's arm.

"Gentlemen, we must dress this soldier's wounds. The Russians themselves would not act otherwise. Care for the wounded is a duty according to the International Code."

The doctor shrugged his shoulders and stammered: "The old man's talking quite stupidly. Where is any International Code respected these days? What has become of our beautiful city? A heap of stinking filth, with thousands of abandoned corpses."

The banker's widow exclaimed impatiently: "Make up your minds one way or the other! The Russians may be here at any moment and all you do is argue. Personally, I'm getting out of this. I've seen nothing and heard nothing!"

The soldier had laboriously raised himself on his elbow and kept turning his eyes, dim with weakness and pain, toward the one who was speaking. His gaze fastened on our lips, as if he were deaf; he did not understand a word of Hungarian and fever made the sense of our argument even harder for him to grasp. Nevertheless, he knew we were deciding whether he should live or die.

His gaze became so embarrassing that soon we fell into a complete silence like a thick fog that obscured all sense of reality.

I no longer had the will to turn my eyes from the blood which seeped faster and faster through his torn uniform.

Suddenly, I had an impression that the ruins over our heads had ceased to exist and that, from heaven, God was watching to see how we were going to pass through this ordeal, almost like death itself. In this extremity, would we consider only a uniform and allow a human life to flow away, drop by drop, under our eyes? I was convinced that God looked on us with pity and, under the weight of His glance, the doctor shook himself abruptly.

"I'll go and get some bandages," he said in a hoarse voice.

He came back a moment later and applied a dressing with rapid, expert movements.

"He's severely wounded in the hip," he told us. "He won't last long. He must be suffering excruciating pain."

9.

THE PASTRY COOK from next door slipped into our building. We received him as if he had come from another planet.

"The Germans have abandoned the street," he announced. "One of them told me they expected an attack and had abandoned their wounded because of the forthcoming battle. The road to the water tap is open at the moment but there's something far more interesting — the Germans have collected a lot of valuable goods in the courthouse. The doors have been forced and we can carry off anything we want."

"We shall go for water," said my father gently, "because that's an absolute necessity. The rest doesn't interest us. We haven't become thieves."

"Thieves?" exclaimed the banker's widow, stung to the quick. "Don't you think that word's a bit strong, Professor? It seems to me that, after months of living like this, we're entitled to look for some compensation!"

My father made no reply and we went to fill our pails. Bearded, yellow, filthy creatures stared at us from the porches, then ventured into the open in ever-increasing numbers. Like cave dwellers assembling in a holiday procession, the multitude, loaded with empty sacks, moved resolutely over mines and corpses toward the courthouse.

Near the baths, the sweetish smell of rotting corpses was so strong that it made me sick and I had to stay outside. My parents entered the building, covering their noses with handkerchiefs. I was uneasy and frightened at the thought that they would have to cross the bridge over the dead man.

And, as I stood there, leaning against the wall, I saw a little old woman go into a stationery store through the front that had been blown away. I watched, fascinated, while she made her choice among the piled-up merchandise, like a fastidious customer. As my parents returned, she came out with her arms loaded with rolls of toilet paper and cellophane for covering jam jars. She disappeared behind a doorway, with a contented expression, like someone who has just made an important purchase to her complete satisfaction.

One after the other, people returned from the courthouse, bent under the weight of their loads. As they reached the narrow lane that led to the bank of the Danube, they flung themselves flat on the ground, as if obeying an order, and crawled the rest of the way home.

We stared, dumbfounded, at the district attorney who, before, had appeared only at the most solemn trials, creeping, dragging himself along the ground, crushed under a heavy carpet. Following him came Ilus, with a blue fox fur about her neck and a bundle in her hand. The banker's wife carried a violin case and a large birdcage. Mr. Radnai brought up the rear, bowed under the weight of three rolls of Oriental rugs.

It was an endless procession of ants pulling or dragging the most diverse objects. They advanced with difficulty among the dead bodies and empty cartridge cases heaped under their feet like dead leaves in an autumn forest.

The sun began to shine. Its sad rays groped feebly among the ruins of the dead town; the watery March light showed the city to be a more ghastly sight than ever.

"We'll have to beware of epidemics," said my father.

We were thinking of the shelters in the cliff

under the royal palace where typhus had raged for nearly a month.

The courtyard looked like a fair. The colonel's wife had five Leica cameras hanging from her arm by their straps. She was discussing the value of her find at the top of her voice. Mr. Radnai was stroking his carpets like a merchant in an Oriental market.

"They're genuine Persians. I'm an expert in that line." Then a long argument arose between him and the district attorney, for the latter claimed his carpet was more valuable.

Ilus had brought back a sack full of silk stockings and, in the kindness of her heart, proceeded to give them away. However, my mother forbade me to accept a pair and so, what with my trousers and my cropped, burned-off hair, I felt betrayed and deserted. Who would have thought that it was precisely my thin, lean-flanked, little-boy appearance that would save me?

At noon, our companions were still busy arranging their treasures when the brooding silence, which frightened us so much, was broken. We heard the tramping of heavy boots and ran into the street to see the Russians arriving.

They marched in disorderly ranks, taking up the entire width of the street, their weapons ready to fire. Their yellow greatcoats were torn and dirty. At each house, a group split off from the main body. This human deluge swept closer and closer to us, and finally a detachment entered our courtyard. In a bellow the commander, a Mongol with slanting eyes, demanded to know if there were any Germans in the house. Several of us nodded our head in the direction of the staircase.

The German was killed on the spot.

From that moment, we realized that what was happening was far different from what we had hoped. The long nightmare of atrocities had begun. Like an apocalyptic flood, sweeping all before it, fresh waves of soldiers invaded the houses. An order from headquarters forbade the burial of the German dead. The corpses of soldiers killed in the fighting, along with those of prisoners massacred point-blank, were thrown into the streets.

10.

THAT NIGHT, someone knocked on the door. We listened, rigid with terror. The thought that it could not be the Russians reassured us a little. They did not knock before entering.

But who could be there? Mr. Radnai went to open the door and drew back in surprise. Three Germans entered. Our faces were as white as if we had seen three ghosts. They were the soldiers who had wanted to blow up the house because of the stolen rations.

"What do you want of us?" gasped the restaurant keeper in a voice like a death rattle.

The captain answered tonelessly: "We want nothing except to ask you a favor — civilian clothes. They are our only, faint hope of escaping. If we are found in uniform, we shall suffer the same fate as the others in front of the house."

At this moment we each discovered exactly what effect Christian teaching had had on our thoughts and actions, and also found out if we could lay claim to any human dignity. We were face to face with the enemy who had destroyed our capital, who were responsible for all the ruins and the fury of the Russians. Here they stood, anxious and faltering. They must have families somewhere in Germany; children, a wife, parents. . . . No doubt they must be praying to see them again. For every soldier has someone waiting for his return; each one follows the orders of his superiors.

All of us must have had the same thoughts, for after a moment or two, we acted on a common impulse. The janitor brought out a suit from his cupboard. "It belonged to my son," he muttered.

Timid eyes were turned toward Mr. Radnai who was now wearing his yellow star. He had the heaviest reckoning against the Germans and his words might have considerable weight with Russians: and a single denunciation would bring us to the gallows.

"I am a Jew," he said in a cold voice. "My entire family was deported. . . ."

Then, silence. Only the yelling of some Russian soldiers reached our ears.

"But, to prove that human kindness still exists, I will let you get away. . . ."

He turned away and, in a few seconds, we found enough clothes to fit out the Germans, who left the house, hugging the walls, their little bundles containing their uniforms under their arms.

That night we could not sleep for the noise of the battle that raged in the distance.

The next day we learned that some of the scattered Germans had regrouped and attempted a counterattack. They had been massacred.

The house was so continually disturbed with the Russians coming and going every minute that Ilus decided to try to cross the Danube and join her family. We went with her as far as the riverbank. There, where once the most imposing houses in the town had stood, nothing remained but a mountain of rubble; the dirty, gray river, jammed with the huge girders of blown-up bridges and piled-up blocks of ice, had completely flooded the wharves.

On the quays Russian soldiers were demanding an astronomical fee for taking passengers across in stolen boats. Ilus came to an understanding with one of them by giving him her wristwatch and an alarm clock. With the child and the soldier, she settled herself in the rowboat and off they went.

We followed them with our eyes. When the boat, with immense difficulty, had reached the swirling eddies in midstream, we noticed some Russian soldiers on the other bank gesticulating wildly and firing into the air to attract attention.

No one understood the reason for their behavior. The boat continued. It had just grazed a pillar of the fallen bridge when a deafening explosion, which shook even us, destroyed the boat, Ilus, the child, and the Russian, who all disappeared under the waves.

That was how we learned that, to keep the entire city from being flooded, the Russians were unblocking the flow of the Danube by blowing up the piers of the bridges. Deeply moved but dry-eyed, we stayed frozen to the spot until the soldiers drove us away.

We returned home — with our hearts in mourning — if one could still say that the mass of ruins, where the German soldier lay rotting under the staircase, was really "home."

Everywhere, along the street, the corpses fastened their glassy eyes upon the living. The stench was becoming unbearable. My parents decided then to leave Budapest as soon as we could and to go to our house in the country.

Just as night fell, the Russians came again — this time to requisition men for forced labor. My father had just gone for water. Mr. Radnai shook his head.

"I'm not going," he said in Russian (for he knew a few words).

All we could understand of the conversation

was the gestures. The Russians had begun to shout. Mr. Radnai replied in a calm voice. Finally, a soldier, purple with rage, drew his revolver and emptied it to the last bullet into the stomach of our companion.

Never shall I forget the expression on his face. He looked astonished, frightened, and angry. He wanted to speak but, when he opened his mouth, only a thick trickle of blood came out. Then he collapsed at our feet, his yellow star stained with blood.

The others went off to their forced labor without further resistance. When we bent over Mr. Radnai, he was already dead.

11.

BEFORE LEAVING Budapest, we wanted to visit the friends living in our villa in the Hüvösvölgy. Our mouths watered at the thought of the food we had stored there and we told ourselves that, after two months, we should at last be able to have enough to eat. However, getting across the city was pretty risky. The Russians might requisition us for forced labor at any moment and, once caught, it would be hard to escape.

Finally, my father and I decided to try our luck. Two months of the siege of Budapest had left their mark on my father; his shoulders were bowed and he had let his beard grow, making his appearance rather pitiful, which was just as well in those days. He armed himself with two empty pails and we made a few holes in his jacket, so he would not strike a discordant note among the ruins and would fit in with the requirements of the new regime. My mother arranged my hair like a boy's, someone found me a pair of glasses, and my right arm was put in a sling to make it look as if I were wounded. Then we set off, trusting in Providence.

We reached the Margit Boulevard, by way of Bem Street, wading up to our ankles in filth and cartridge cases. Russian soldiers were loitering all along the sidewalks. In one place they had rounded up casual passers-by and pressed them into forced labor gangs, but they let us pass without bothering us. What use could an old man laden with pails and a wounded boy have been in cleaning up the ruins? Our route took us by a big movie house; they were just bringing out some dead horses. Near Szenater Square there were a great many dead German soldiers. Here, two days before, they had attempted a breakthrough and were all mown down; the streetcar tracks were running with their blood.

Suddenly, I put my foot on something soft. It was a human arm. Torn from its trunk, it still wore the German uniform; a wedding ring gleamed on one finger. My teeth chattered with horror. After this, I walked with my eyes pinned to the ground. Near the Budagyongye streetcar stop a soldier lay on his stomach, arms outstretched as if crucified. Beside his inert right hand, the ground was strewn with photographs.

Had he, in his final agony, tried to send a last message to his family by staring at their pictures? It was as if, at the Budagyongye stop, he were waiting for the coming of some celestial, redeeming streetcar. His soul seemed already far away from that body abandoned on the pavement.

There was less destruction in the next district we went through; the Russians had occupied these residential streets quickly. It was here we had had to turn back two months ago, two months which seemed to us more like twenty years.

As we approached the villa, the streets became more and more familiar. If the house were still intact, if some of our stores yet remained, our worries would be over. And, besides, there were those good friends who must have been so anxious about us. We were faint with hunger.

At last we came within sight of the house. What a relief! The bombardment had spared it. We went through the garden gate. On the terrace were some tables and chairs. We entered the hall, and the sound of voices reached us from a distance. Like blind people, we followed the sound which guided us to the kitchen. Our friends were all there, eating. They were gathered around a properly laid table; a delicious smell wafted through the room. Aunt Julia, a tall, stout lady, froze at the sight of us; the soup spilled from her spoon and she challenged hoarsely: "What, you aren't dead, all of you?"

"We're still alive," I answered shyly, almost apologetically.

It took them some time to recover from their astonishment but, finally, they offered us seats at the table.

"Would you like something to eat, darling?" inquired Aunt Julia and the word "darling" fell from her lips almost like a curse. She resented our being alive. She had grown used to the idea of our death — perhaps she had even mourned us a little — and now she was angry to have wept for nothing.

"We watched the bombing of the Danube from the terrace," said one of the boys, his lips all smeared with grease.

They watched from the terrace, I thought, and the mouthful of soup suddenly turned bitter. My father was silent.

Later, as we talked about our two months of famine in the cellar, he remarked: "We'll take a few provisions with us."

"Provisions?" Aunt Julia blazed. "My dear man, that's impossible, we've absolutely nothing left. We've used up almost all the food. We needed a great deal for my big family. After all, one can't ration youngsters when they're growing. As we'd been refugees since Kolozsvar, our own provisions had almost run out."

Without a word, we got up and proceeded to inspect the other rooms. The beds were made with our monogrammed sheets and covered with our blankets.

"We are saving our own," explained Aunt Julia, fussing about. "After all, my dear, we thought you were all dead and didn't need anything any more."

"Only a coffin," added my father drily.

"There isn't much left of your silver," the dear lady explained. "The contents of your cases decreased every time the Russians visited us. They've taken nearly all of it."

We packed up what remained. Barely six pounds of flour were left of two great sackfuls. But there were still some sugar and a few cans of food. Tonight we could prepare a real feast.

We started home with empty hearts and weary bodies. A blazing sun slanted its rays over the dead city that lay before us. We shuddered at the evidence of the eternal renewal of spring; green shoots already sprouted between the two fingers of a corpse; the gentle grass pushed aside the cartridge cases scattered on the ground.

The behavior of our friends fitted in well with the current atmosphere of the capital.

It was neither repellent nor inconceivable. All ethical ideas had been turned upside down in the ruined city. Vice counted as virtue and hard hearts had more chance of survival than tender ones.

A truck overtook us, loaded with men dressed in leather jackets and armed with tommy guns. Their vehicle jolted slightly as it ran over a dead body. Ghostlike creatures passed us on the sidewalk; they seemed to be in disguise. It was as if all of us were characters in some Shakespearean drama, outlaws living on the edge of the normal world.

The tenants in our bombed house in Buda were anxiously watching for our return. They told us they had seen a number of Russian women in uniform in the streets, who had said, in commiseration, that Budapest was in a worse state than Stalingrad. We, too, had seen these Russian women soldiers. They wore large rubber brassières and were heavy-set, with legs like pillars, and looked strong enough to lift an armored tank on their shoulders.

Life became more and more difficult; every day brought a fresh problem. The bomb that had pierced my piano was still embedded in the parquet; no one dared touch it. The library had neither doors nor windows; breezes blew the manuscripts about, scattering the torn pages. The Russian soldiers had dirtied the armchairs in the living room. We left everything as it was. It was impossible to move in again. Wherever we went — in our apartment or in the open street — we found rubble and excrement. So we decided to leave Budapest and go to live in our little country villa in Transdanubia.

Since there were no trains running on this side of the Danube, we had to begin by crossing over to Pest. We would then cross back again at a point lower down. The Germans had blown up all the bridges but at the railroad station we learned there was a pontoon bridge at Baja, below the capital.

At the station, we succeeded in slipping into a cattle car. We swept out the heap of dried dung as best we could and waited patiently along with a crowd of about three thousand people who had waited with us since the morning. Toward eleven at night, it became obvious that the train would not leave. Teeth chattering, and ravenously hungry, the crowd descended on the little village of Soroksar seeking shelter for the night. The panic-stricken peasants barricaded themselves in their houses and shouted from the windows that they had nothing left either, that the enemy had carried off everything, even their pillows. Nevertheless, a kindly carpenter took pity on us and let us sleep in his workshop. We stretched out on a bed of shavings. At dawn, we quenched our thirst at his well before returning to the station.

That day, the Russians ordered us into a different train. We asked a railway employee if he knew what they were going to do and whether we would go at all.

He shrugged his shoulders. "I have no idea!"

Meanwhile, our freight car was filled to bursting with Russian soldiers and Russian women.

"It's a good sign," said a white-faced man who was carrying a small child in a knapsack. "With Russians on board, the train will probably leave."

A young mother with four children, a heavily made-up middle-aged woman, and an old bearded gentleman were traveling with us. We squeezed together into a corner of the car to leave as much room as possible for the soldiers and to escape their attention. The crowded train waited a few more hours, then, after a sudden violent jolt, it slowly began to move.

There was a commotion among the people left behind in the station and some of them tried to jump on at the last minute, shouting, and clutching at every available handhold.

The train was moving slowly toward a loading platform which stood very close to the track. Suddenly, a man darted from the crowd and leapt on the step of a coach, reserved for the Russian army, which was traveling empty, with locked doors. He shook the handle of the door frantically, his face convulsed with the effort, but in vain. Suddenly the crowd began to yell like one man; the loading platform was so close to the tracks that anyone standing on the step would inevitably be swept off.

The man kept struggling with the door and did not notice the danger until the cement wall caught him and sent him spinning against the side of the coach. The crowd froze in horrified silence. Above the metallic rattle of the train, one could distinctly hear the cracking of bones. With his face purple and swollen and blood spurting in gushes from his mouth, the human top lifted himself up, then fell back. It seemed that, at last, he was going to fall to the ground. But the wall would not let him go and continued to mangle him for another twenty yards.

A great shout of pain and rebellion rose from the watching crowd. They raised their fists to heaven and screamed: "Oh God, how can You permit a human being to be so mangled by a stone?" Some Russian soldiers, leaning out of one of the compartments, tried to drag the victim in. Women sobbed and wrung their hands; tears ran down the faces of hardened men. A Russian soldier covered his eyes and fired into the air as if to attract the attention of a divine power. At that moment we were no longer victors and vanquished; the cruel fate of one nameless Hungarian had aroused feelings of pity and horror in all of us. Upon reaching

82

the end of the loading platform, the mangled man, unconscious now, dropped beside the track like a yellow, bloodstained rag. The train moved around a curve. We were left numb and shattered by the tragic episode.

The convoy proceeded at a speed of fifteen or twenty miles an hour. Those riding on the roof of the train were roasted by day and frozen by night. After twenty-four hours we were all dying of hunger and thirst. The first night in that cattle train was a terrible ordeal.

At one point, the Russian soldiers handed a bottle of wine to the mother of the four children. Smiling, but threatening her with their revolvers, they forced her to drink.

Her little five-year-old girl stretched out her arms.

"Mummy, I'm thirsty, too. . . ."

The mother held the bottle away from the child but the Russian, still pointing his revolver, ordered: "Give some to your children, too!"

He made the three older ones drink, sparing only the baby. Naturally, they all became drunk. The children were sick and the mother spent the night singing. She almost began to dance, to the huge delight of the Russian soldiers who were doubled up with laughter. No one dared mention thirst again.

We were sitting on our knapsacks in the farthest corner of the car. A soldier, stretched out in front of us, had propped his shoulder on my father's foot; all night long my father dared not withdraw it.

We welcomed the dawn with relief, and our thoughts turned to our little house in the country, that haven of peace and serenity which we were now nearing. Should we find it intact or see nothing but a heap of ruins?

Toward noon, the news spread that the train, instead of going to Baja, would take us into Russia by way of Rumania. It was the pale man who launched this rumor, assuring us that the Russian soldiers on the train were going home on leave. From that moment on we thought only of escape. But the train, which up to then had crawled as slowly as a turtle, suddenly speeded up. The soldiers began to sing and to fire shots through the windows.

During the afternoon, we no longer knew whether we were free travelers or deported prisoners. In the evening, the train slowed down and stopped at a little, unknown village. We implored the Russians to let us get off to satisfy certain natural needs. To avoid suspicion, we left all our luggage in the train before disappearing into the bushes, which luckily were thick just there. A quarter of an hour later, we heard shouts and rifle shots warning us the train was leaving. But no one went back.

To this very day, I do not know whether our fears were well-founded or not. Yet, we dared not risk finding ourselves in a Siberian internment camp at the end of the trip.

After a brief consultation, our whole group of refugees continued the journey on foot. A peasant informed us that Baja was about thirty-six miles away.

It took three days to get there. The first night a peasant took us into his house; the other two we spent in stables. For food we had bread and milk. About seven on the third evening, we arrived at Baja Station where a railwayman told us how we might cross the Danube.

"A Bulgarian military train is leaving the station in half an hour, carrying guns on flat cars. Perhaps you can climb onto it. It's your only chance — only army convoys can use the pontoon bridge."

Thanking him, we examined the train standing in the station. It was an impressive sight, for it seemed impossible that the wheels could support the weight of such huge cannons. A Bulgarian soldier, rifle in hand, was pacing up and down the platform. My father explained to him in German that it had taken us five days to accomplish a journey which would normally have taken five hours and, if we could not reach our house on the other side of the river, we were lost; we no longer had enough money or strength to retrace the hard road back.

The Bulgarian understood and thought it over for a considerable time. He was a thin boy not more than twenty. But his back was already slightly bent, as if destiny had imposed an excessive weight on his generation.

He looked at us again very carefully and motioned us to join him on the train.

"How much do I owe you?" inquired my father.

"Nothing," he said gently, as he helped my mother and me to climb on the train. "Whatever happens, keep calm. I'll fix things with my friends."

Seated on a gun carriage, we proceeded, once again, to wait. Some twenty minutes later, about fifteen Bulgarian soldiers joined us and lay down on the wooden floor without taking any notice of us.

The train moved off. It soon reached the bridge. But could it be called a bridge, this collection of planks which seemed absurdly fragile and which was only just as wide as the gauge of the tracks? We were convinced that our days would end at the bottom of the Danube, along with the cannons. The heavily loaded convoy launched itself cautiously onto the floating bridge; the sullen water swirled noisily, and the wind that swept down the great river tore at our hair. Then the soldiers began to sing. Carried by those male voices, the melody echoed sadly through the night. All about us, the water splashed and gurgled as the train rolled slowly on, wavering slightly from side to side.

The moment drew us all together, shivering civilians and foreign soldiers perched alike on gun carriages two feet above the Danube in the starless night, and created an atmosphere that was almost sublime.

One might have thought that this journey would take us into eternity, strange exiles that we were, rejected by both shores. The song rose higher and higher, as if beating on the gates of heaven to implore admission for a handful of souls whose bodies would remain with the cannons, buried deep in mud.

A sudden jolt, and the train laboriously began to climb a slope. We had reached the other bank.

In the morning, we thanked the soldiers for their kindness and set off along the main road on the last stage of our journey. After a few brief halts and three days' walking, we reached our goal. Our house was intact and the great lake of Balaton lay calm and blue at the foot of the green hills, as if it wished to know nothing of the tragic events that had taken place on its shores.

12.

CHAPTER

FOR THREE YEARS we lived modestly in our little country house. We had gotten more or less used to our new circumstances until political persecution began to eliminate people all around us like a smallpox epidemic. We decided to stake all we had on getting across the frontier before it was too late.

The day before our departure I set off on my bicycle for a distant village where no one knew me. I went into the little church, all golden in the autumn sunlight, to say a prayer. Since then, I have visited the most beautiful cathedrals in Europe but they cannot make me forget that simple little house of God. The saints, painted by some unsophisticated hand, smiled down at me from the white walls; an old peasant woman was decorating the altar with fresh flowers, and toothlessly muttering prayers. As I knelt in the last bench, I noticed that the parish priest was sitting in the confessional. Why did that let loose such a flood of violent feeling? A sudden shock ran through me as if I had touched a live wire, reviving all my memories at once: our life in the cellar, the marriage of Eve and Gabriel, the death of brave Pista. And now, tomorrow, we would leave our beloved refuge. Sometimes fate makes the most peaceful citizen assume a heroic role. Almost without knowing what I was doing I went to kneel inside the confessional.

The priest looked at me quickly, then covered his eyes with his hand. He was still young and very pale.

"Father," I whispered, "I hadn't expected to make my Confession. I am not prepared; I haven't thought about my sins. Something stronger than I drives me to confide in you. If you knew me, I would not tell you that tomorrow I am leaving with my family to cross the frontier. I should be too much afraid of compromising you. But I have come a long way and I came in here by chance. So I can tell you what we are about to do.

"I'm terribly frightened. I pray, but it's no use. There's nothing but a great blank behind my words. Why should God listen to me? My voice is so feeble, my appeal can't possibly reach Him. Besides, I've sinned, because I've cried about all sorts of insignificant things during the last three years. While men have been dying all around me, I've been resentful because there haven't been any parties for me, because I've never been able to go anywhere, dressed in white and flushed with excitement. The dead sit by my bed at night and, instead of dreams, I have horrible visions. In the morning I don't know whether they are nightmares or whether the dead really do appear to drag me into their world of shadows.

"Father, I've rebelled at not having known what it's like to be young and carefree. My happy childhood has been so completely blotted out of my mind that I can't recall it even in scraps. All is darkness and fear. When someone stops in front of our house, I imagine it's the police. If I hear footsteps behind me, I think I'm being followed. All this is only illusion, but it tortures me. I would have liked so much to be happy. . . ."

He answered: "I don't know who you are nor where you come from. One person among a hundred thousand. It's as if you spoke in their name to us all. If you succeed in crossing the frontier, perhaps it will be your duty to tell what has happened in this country. But remember this: Justice and charity come before everything. In any case, what happens to us here on earth is not very important, since our true life is waiting for us above. I shall not give you any penance, but I charge you to pray every day with a deep faith. And I absolve you in the name of the Father and of the Son and of the Holy Ghost."

The little old woman had finished her pious task and was praying, kneeling beneath the oil lamp that burned before the altar. I left the church. The sun was setting and the shadow of the Cross had grown so long that it seemed to stretch into the distance and cover the whole countryside.

Night had already fallen when I reached home. It was raining, and the handle of the garden gate was so cold that it made me shiver to touch it.

"Where have you been?" my father asked as he came to meet me.

"I went for a ride," I answered evasively. Then I sat down on a chair, staring straight in front of me. . . .

My father held some papers in his hand; my mother was packing clothes into a suitcase. The doors of the closets were wide open and, in one corner, stood a packing case with its lid raised, half-filled with books.

"When do we go?" I asked with a little shudder at the thought of leaving the house in the pouring rain.

"Tomorrow night, my child," answered my

mother in a voice that sounded reproachful to me.

I huddled near the stove without strength or wish to stir. The warmth had made me torpid and I felt as if I were watching a film in which my parents were moving about on a gigantic screen. It was incredible, the number of belongings we had!

When we arrived, three years ago, we had had to work like Western pioneers settling on virgin soil. We had nailed up the broken doors. We had gathered feathers, one by one, to stuff the burst pillows; we had collected kitchen utensils that had been thrown out into the garden behind the house. It was there, too, that we had found our silver buried in the earth.

The peasants had, at first, regarded us with suspicion, as if we were not human beings but ghosts who had refused to vanish after an occult seance. When they passed us, you could see that they wanted to reach out and touch us, and they whispered behind our backs, with a mixture of fear and respect, that we were survivors from the siege of Budapest. Eventually they had grown used to the idea that we were alive and they had become more friendly. One day, the man who sold us milk before the war had brought us a setting hen and some eggs.

"How you've grown, young lady!" he had told me. I was astonished then to realize that

I had grown taller in our cellar, instead of dying.

From time to time, other people arrived from Budapest. They were starved creatures, most of whom had made the journey on the roof of a train. With eyes starting from their sockets, they had told us hideous stories of what happened when warm weather came; of the corpses which had rotted under the pitiless sun. We fell silent then, as if ashamed of our inability to feel terror or shock or disgust.

Sometimes I was seized by an inner fear that was purely physical. At such moments, I had nothing in common with my body.

The days that had gone by since the siege had cheated and betrayed me. I had left the cellar filled with ardent hope. A child had died there. She began life again as an adult. I wanted someone else to be glad I was alive. But men were interested in no one but themselves, and the sun caressed my thin arms and pale face with as much indifference as if I had been a blade of grass. Time drifted by while I contemplated the lake and waited for the unknown man who would love me. Nothing happened but the passing of the seasons.

When my parents announced that we were going to cross the frontier, I had a new surge of hope. Perhaps, at last, life would begin.

As I looked about me, I wondered what I

could take away. Before the siege, I had been given a beautiful long silk nightgown. It was my first piece of feminine lingerie and I had never worn it. I decided to take it with me.

"What will become of the dog?" I asked suddenly.

At this question, my mother stopped dead, as if I had struck her.

The dog must have realized we were talking about him, for he came out of the corner where he had been lying and wagged his tail. He belonged to no definite breed. He was a mongrel but infinitely charming and intelligent. Each of his movements showed modesty, as if he wished to apologize for his ugliness. He watched us attentively and seemed to smile. He must have been convinced that we were saying very nice things about him.

Betraying a dog is even more cruel than betraying a human being, for he does not understand what is going on and can judge only by voice and expression. If you say the meanest things to him in a gentle voice and with a smile, he licks your hand gratefully. I did not want to betray our poor dog.

"What will become of the dog?" I repeated in an irritable, sharp voice, so that he would know that something threatened him. But he kept on wagging his tail.

"We'll have to give him to the lawyer," said my mother, thinking out loud. But no sooner had the words slipped out than she realized this was impossible, for we could not mention our departure to anyone. How then could we give away the poor dog?

The question remained unsolved. But it never stopped haunting us through all the bustle of packing.

I went to the closet and looked through my possessions. I had a summer dress of white handwoven linen which I did not need to take for it was November and raining. I had another dress of claret-colored velvet, made from a drawing-room curtain. How else could one have any clothes at that time? This dress invariably reminded me of the curtains and I had never gotten used to wearing it. There were also the heavy sweater and skirt I wore every day and my school uniform, which had been ridiculously short and tight across my chest. I had some high-heeled shoes that I had bought for the village dance. Tomorrow we should have to walk. I needed only the low shoes I usually wore. At the back of the closet lay the notebooks in which I had kept my diary of the siege. Should I take them or leave them behind? I still had time to decide, a whole night in which to think it over.

That night we went late to bed. The family was packing as conscientiously as if we were setting off on a legitimate journey. The electric light became gradually fainter and the curtains were carefully drawn so that no one could see in from outside.

Why did everything seem so strange and far away, as if I had no connection with the minutes I was living through? My mother's features looked more and more hollow in the lamplight. Suddenly I realized that everything she had packed into the suitcase would have to go back into the closets.

I watched this final farewell to our possessions and felt sorry for my parents. The road that would take us into the unknown tomorrow would be a harsh ordeal for them. And for me? I should have to be reborn to be capable of feeling anything. At the moment, I was sunk in a drowsy and stubborn inertia. The dog slept in his corner.

"What should I do with the alarm clock?" asked my mother, as if incapable of making a decision. "Should we take it with us, too?"

"I don't know," I replied.

My mother was holding a little lace collar in her hand.

"This came from Brussels," she said. "I kept it all through the siege. I'm not going to leave it for *them*."

"*Do* go to bed!" It was my father's voice from the next room. However, he knew perfectly well that his injunction was quite pointless at the moment.

Finally we went to bed. My pillow had become hard; it seemed to have become hostile. Every time I moved, my heart fluttered anxiously. I thrashed about on my bed. I sat up. Was I still alive?

The morning seemed brutally real. Objects recovered their ordinary shapes and colors; even words had more meaning than they had had during the night. Only everything was heavier than usual. I could hardly hold my cup of coffee; all weight seemed concentrated there. My mother returned from the garden where she had gone to feed the hens and rabbits. We had kept them ever since we came to live in the country. They had been a necessity; now they would be left to fate.

I could not swallow my bread. A lump grew in my throat every time I tried to eat. We must cook something for lunch. A chicken, for instance, so as to leave one less behind. I was too weary to catch one of the fluttering creatures. They escaped with a shrill cackling. In the end I gave up; the noise got on my nerves.

Toward noon I asked in a detached voice: "Shall we have a guide?"

"Yes," replied my father. "All we have to do is to meet him on time."

"Where?"

"At the appointed place."

"Which town? Which village?"

"Better for you not to know."

It so happened that one of the lawyer's daughters turned up during the afternoon. She behaved as if it were still peacetime. She had come just to gossip; she was gay and we revolved about her, like puppets dancing on strings. She and I planned to meet again in two days: I took a long time deciding the exact hour for she proposed five o'clock and I, a quarter past. I acted as if a difference of fifteen minutes was immensely important. I was satisfied when, at last, she accepted my choice.

"But above all, don't keep me waiting," she said laughing.

Then she told us that her father knew he was "under observation"; that often they were disturbed at night, just to see if they were at home.

"We're quite used to it now," she added, laughing again. But her laughter got on my nerves, for it rang false, and I noticed that her eyes remained serious. The nose was a neutral point between a laughing mouth and chin and a serious forehead and eyes. What would happen if I were to tell her that, a few hours from now, we should no longer be here? This thought excited me to such a pitch that I ran out into the garden for a moment, holding my face up to the wind to cool the inner fire that burned my cheeks. If someone were beside me then, even if he were a perfect stranger,

I would have told him that, in a few hours, we were setting off to cross the frontier. I longed to share the secret that weighed on me. The dog rubbed himself against my legs. He had followed me, arching his back like a cat.

I went back indoors, shivering. Our guest was taking her leave. She kissed me, and insisted: "Don't forget — day after tomorrow at quarter past five."

We held our breath until we heard the creak of the garden gate.

"What luck she didn't stay longer," my mother said at last. And she opened the door of a closet as if she were going to let out someone who had been hiding there.

My father cautiously looked at his watch.

"The train leaves at six o'clock and it is now five minutes past four. It's time to get ready."

I rushed to fetch the clothes I was taking with me. After putting on several layers of underwear, the nightgown, well tucked up, was fastened over them with safety pins, along with the velvet dress. Over the whole I slipped my sweater and everyday skirt. It gave me a funny feeling to walk about padded like that. I knew then how a very fat woman must feel in a crowded streetcar on a hot day. My parents were dressed in the same way, for we could not carry any luggage, not even a little bag of food. What would people say? We should have eaten something before we left but not one of us could swallow a bite.

The dog who, up to then, had been very nervous, sat down on the doorstep, wagging his tail and showing his narrow gums. He seemed to be smiling in a way that meant: "I'm the first one ready. Now we can go!"

Once again I was overcome by a feeling of loneliness. No one would say good-bye to me, no one would wait for me by the hedge to give me a farewell kiss as he swore to be eternally faithful. I had no one with whom I could arrange a system of corresponding in code, no one whom I could hope to meet again in after years.

I stood stock still by the closet. I did not cry. The story was so inhuman that it did not leave the smallest loophole for escape, even for a tear. Now I was anxious only to go and go quickly. Every minute spent between those walls was making me weaker. My parents were not yet completely dressed. I waited. Before beginning this journey into the unknown, I wanted to recall certain scenes. I should have liked to take with me the memory of a few faces at least. But there was not one that lived within me and it was then that I suddenly remembered the notebooks with my diary of the siege. I pulled them hastily from the cupboard, and tore out the pages covered with small, cramped writing. I folded them up and divided them among my pockets.

My mother was struggling to put her fur coat on over several layers of dresses. Her movements also were severely hindered by all the clothes. At that moment some strange devil in me asked, What is the point? Why must we go?

Ever since we had left the cellar, the whole family had been numb with fear. My parents had never spoken of it, as if, by silence, they could shield me from fate. "This is the last chance to try to make the crossing," said my father quietly. Thus, involuntarily, he put an end to an argument, which, in fact, had never begun.

I dared to suggest: "Your expression gives you away. You ought to change it; I see fear in your eyes."

"Nonsense," retorted my mother, without conviction. She clutched the table as if she wanted to take it with her. The whole house had an air of consternation. Dragged by its own weight, the closet door swung open of its own accord. A crust of bread and a pitcher half full of water remained on the table.

My mother wrapped the bread in a napkin. "So it won't dry out," she said, by way of excuse. Everywhere, order reigned; a meticulous order, a lifeless order, as if the house were already abandoned. Yet there we still were, swollen with clothes, undecided. Anyone might have come in then and carried on the life we had led between these walls. But would anyone have wanted such a life?

As we went out, we left the light on and locked the door behind us.

"Let's keep the key," my mother suggested. "We might still come back."

"If our plans succeed, we shan't need the key. And, if they fail, we shan't need it either. . . ."

My father spoke quietly and flatly, as if reciting this phrase for the hundredth time. Then, with a sweeping gesture, he hurled the key into the garden, invisible in the darkness. We strained our ears but we did not hear even the little clink of its fall. It was as if an invisible hand had deftly caught the key in full flight.

Our next movements had been minutely planned for weeks. We knew exactly what answers to give if anyone questioned us. First of all, we would go to the station. We would buy tickets only to the next town, so that the ticket agent could not tell any one where we were going. At the next station, my father planned to buy tickets as far as the frontier. If, on the train, a patrol asked us why we were going to Ováros, we would talk about Aunt Charlotte, a distant relative who lived there and who had invited us. When we arrived at Ováros, we would try to leave the train as inconspicuously as possible and go to the suburbs where the guide lived. We would follow him, and he would take us as far as the station of the first Austrian village. Then, Vienna. We had enough money to pay the guide and to buy two thousand Austrian schillings. After that, we would see. Such was our plan. There was nothing to do now except take care that everything happened as arranged so that we would not lose control of events and of ourselves.

We walked slowly down the highway. It was only five o'clock but it was already dark and was raining. The dog bounded along in front of us. He ran ahead, then stopped and retraced his steps to make certain he had not lost us. My father walked with difficulty; he could not see well in the dark. My mother held my arm. I was perspiring. My layers of clothes stifled me.

We arrived at the station.

In the distance, the train was approaching with an ever-increasing rumble. At last it came into the station. We climbed the steep iron steps to the compartment. The dog made despairing leaps to follow us and had just managed to hoist himself onto the lowest step when another passenger, an elderly man who was impatient to climb aboard, brutally kicked him off. Not in the least discouraged, the dog jumped up again, but the doors were already shut. Standing in the corridor, I could not manage to open the window; it was jammed, or too stiff. I pulled it with all my might and felt one of my dresses split, while sweat began to trickle down my back and tears run down my chin. I pressed my face against the glass so that no one would notice that I was crying, and, in despair, with blurred eyes stared at the deserted dog through the misted pane.

The train was moving and the dog was barking; he began to run along the platform beside the coach. His thin, ugly little paws carried him at breakneck speed and I had the impression that he was catching up, and would leap onto the carriage step. But he grew smaller and smaller; already he had stopped barking, he had only strength enough to run. Then he was no more than a little speck. The train had left the station and was rolling between dark fields.

I went into the compartment. Besides my parents three people were sitting in it: two men and a woman. The silence was complete: one could hear only the rumble of the wheels. Before the war, these coaches had been enlivened by the chatter of the passengers. Now, no one dared to start a conversation. Any sentence might be dangerous and it was impossible to know who might be a police spy. The silent journey had something frightening about it. I had not brought a book. Outside, the darkness hid everything. I closed my eyes and leaned my head against the back of the seat. The eyes of the woman sitting opposite me burned through my closed lids. I decided to stare at her in return; it was the only way to make her turn her head away.

The conductor appeared, and he punched our tickets without saying a word.

"How many minutes do we stop at Bétatelep?" inquired my father.

"We don't stop there at all," replied the conductor, suddenly becoming more talkative. "Two days ago they cut out that stop for the evening train."

The woman with the piercing eyes began to look at us with interest. This time, it was my mother who freed us from our delicate situation, by saying to my father: "Then it would be better to stop and see them on the way back from Óváros and not to break our journey now. Can't you buy tickets as far as that?"

"Is it possible to extend our tickets to Óváros?" asked my father.

The conductor nodded his head and dug out of his pouch a book of tickets separated by sheets of carbon paper. How complicated it is to buy a ticket on the train! The conductor had to make three separate entries but, finally, everything was arranged and my father put the tickets in his pocket. We would all have liked to take off our coats but we did not dare, for the others would then see our heavily padded shapes. There was nothing to do but sit in silence, motionless with suspense.

"I believe it has stopped raining," began my mother, after an endless time.

My father nodded and let his cigar ash drop on his overcoat. He promptly brushed it off with scrupulous care. The train grew emptier and emptier as it neared the frontier town. The disagreeable woman began to collect her belongings, as did the men. It was only then that we realized they were traveling together. They had not spoken; now they had gone.

My father consulted his watch.

"The train's on time," he affirmed.

We went out into the corridor. The train slowed to a stop in the station of Ováros. We were the only people to get off, which was far from reassuring. It was half past nine. Having perspired on the train, we now shivered in the wind and the moonlight. A railroad worker ran along the tracks, a red lantern in his hand.

"If they ask us anything — Aunt Charlotte!" repeated my father, tickets in hand, as we made our way to the exit. Finally, we were outside the station, in an almost deserted street. Two policemen watched us from the sidewalk opposite.

"Don't turn around," said my father. "Walk faster."

We followed him for he knew the way. He

had prepared our flight well. We left the center of town and went farther and farther away from it through a maze of narrow, dimly lit streets. When we reached the outskirts, my father knocked on the door of a house with darkened windows. The door opened almost at once and a warm, unpleasant smell assailed our nostrils. A woman ushered us in and led us to a room lit by a bright strong bulb. The curtains were carefully drawn. I looked hastily about. On a stove that gave off an infernal heat was a pot reeking of onions. At the table a fat man was busy eating. He did not get up when we came in but merely motioned us to sit.

"It's off for tonight!" he said between spoonfuls. His chin was greasy and I should have liked to see his eyes but they were fixed on his soup.

"But why?" asked my father, in consternation.

The man at last decided to look at us. "Because of the moon, of course. Shines too bright. Lights up everything. Can't possibly set off like that. Anyway, I don't want to risk my skin."

The woman set another dish on the table. I scrutinized the face of the guide, and listened so intensely to his explanations that the meaning of the sentences escaped me. I understood only one thing; it was all off. Perhaps tomorrow. It didn't concern him; he had no control over the moon. Then he made us understand that we must go away and return at half past nine the following night.

"But where can we spend the night and all day tomorrow?" asked my father. "We can't go to a hotel. The police would be warned at once."

He waited for the guide to suggest our spending the night there. But the greasy-chinned peasant was positive and peremptory; he had undertaken to take us across the frontier. Period. No question of staying in his house; the police made too many searches and had been keeping their eye on him for some time. He would make the trip only once or twice again, no more. This kind of business was becoming too dangerous.

His wife added in a flat voice: "You'd better go at once. Come back tomorrow night."

We had to make up our minds. But where to go? I was hungry.

"Could you give me a little water?" I said, in hopes of being offered something to eat.

Impatiently, the woman ran some water into a thick-rimmed cup and thrust it into my hands. I took only two sips. The water was tepid and smelled of disinfectant.

13.

A FEW MOMENTS LATER, we were back in the street once more. Right away we had to start walking in a definite direction, as if we knew where we were going. Strollers were suspect, and if we were asked for explanations, all would be lost. So we set off with firm, decisive steps, like people afraid of being late for an appointment.

"Where are we going?" I asked, panting.

The cold air I breathed in cut like a knife.

"There may still be one chance," said my father. "But, if that fails, there's nothing to do but take the train again and keep traveling until tomorrow evening. Impossible to go to a hotel, and station waiting rooms are too often raided by the police."

We followed unknown streets and arrived at last in front of a church. My father climbed the steps and we followed him. The heavy door was not locked. We pushed it open. In dense shadow, the sanctuary lamp gave out a faint glimmer before the invisible altar. Exhausted, my mother and I sank down in the last row of benches. As for my father, he disappeared. Should we sit here until daylight? And what should we do all tomorrow? We could not stay in a church for twenty-four hours. I ought to have prayed then, but I hadn't the strength. I was cold, I was hungry, I was sleepy.

My father returned and touched us on the shoulder. "Come," he whispered.

We followed him down the nave into the sacristy. Complete darkness reigned. But a gleam that filtered through the crack of a door revealed a priest standing in front of us. He shook hands with us and invited us to follow him. He spoke in a low voice.

"Be very careful, I implore you, and crouch well down, the moment you enter the room where we are going. The window has no curtains and a street lamp shines in from outside. The house opposite is a police station and the policemen can see everything that goes on. If we should hang up a curtain, it would rouse their curiosity."

I wanted to look at the priest's face so as to judge how much charity and how much fear there was in him; but he had no face. He opened the door for us and we went into the room, stooping as much as possible. The street lamp swayed in the wind and its shadow swung to and fro on the wall. We sat down on the floor.

"We can stay here until tomorrow evening," my father explained.

"How did you arrange this?" asked my mother.

But the question remained unanswered.

"We must get undressed," I said.

"Only our coats," replied my father.

Never had I imagined it would be so difficult to take off a coat while squatting on the floor. We helped each other as best we could. My father was elderly and had high blood pressure, but he did not complain. Outside, the wind redoubled its violence. The street lamp slanted its beam on the opposite wall, sent it dancing up to the ceiling where it disappeared in a flash; then, a moment later, the whole process began again. I became as giddy as if I had been on a ship. I closed my eyes but the light hurt me, even through my eyelids. A strange sensation of seasickness came over me. My sweat-soaked clothes stifled me and a sick feeling dragged me down to the land of nightmares. I wanted to open my eyes but the luminous pendulum that swung ever faster and wider paralyzed me. Then, in the dizzy vortex of anguish and drowsiness, a mouth appeared to me: a mouth with curving lips. Whose mouth was it and where had I seen it so clearly that I was sure I knew it? The mouth smiled and spoke to me, but I could not hear the words.

The night of torture dragged on. At one point, we were already crossing the frontier, but the swinging of the lamp brought me back to reality. It was two o'clock in the morning. My parents were asleep. Whose mouth was it? Sleep overcame me once more. I was running along a dark road. A dead man came to meet me, one of those who had lain in front of our house in Budapest. He beckoned to me and smiled.

"They've stolen the wedding ring off my finger," he told me, gaily. "I'm going to reclaim it from the thief. No doubt he'll give me back my arm, too."

I noticed then that he had lost an arm and that a flower was growing out of the wound, getting bigger and bigger, until it finally hid the dead man's face.

At last it was daylight. Our strength came back just as, on the battlefield, dawn revives a wounded man enough so that he can drag himself, crawling, toward a village.

Crawling like that, we left the room.

In the passage, we stood upright and walked along to a narrow alcove where we found what we needed to make a sketchy toilet. We had to keep on all our clothes. Soon after, we were once more squatting in the room where we had spent the night. An old priest, with an impassive face, brought us some coffee. He set the cups on the floor as if that were the natural place to put them. He did not speak, and behaved as if he scarcely noticed us. Time passed with maddening slowness. Heaven grant there would be no moon that night! So far, the weather was cold and rainy, the sky muffled and gray.

Hours of not moving; then, again — night. The dance of the street lamp began again. Six o'clock. After an interminable wait, it was finally eight. I hid my face in my hands to shield my eyes from the light. I felt I was pressing my face against a stranger's hand. The feeling was not new to me, but whose hand was it and when had it stroked my face before?

At nine, we crept out of the room. The priest stood in the dusk and nodded good-bye. First through the sacristy, then, again, the church. The wan light of the sanctuary lamp drew a faint red veil before my eyes. We were returned to the night. As we made our way, we anxiously scanned the sky. The thick clouds were so low that they seemed near enough to touch.

The door of the guide's house opened at the first knock. This time, the couple was more friendly. The wife was making mulled wine for us.

"Wine? Now?" my father asked, incredulously.

"I make everyone have some before we start," said the guide, with a grin. "Gives 'em strength and raises their morale. I can't undertake anything with people who are afraid. And everyone is afraid on an empty stomach, even me. So let's drink."

He emptied a great mug of steaming wine. I raised mine to my lips and tasted it. It was spiced and scalding. But my palate soon became accustomed to it and I emptied my mug avidly and resolutely. The drink warmed our tired, famished bodies as if new blood had been injected into them. The room suddenly looked larger and the guide's face rounder.

"I've drunk it all," I said thickly, with a broad grin.

I felt that my mouth was split to the ears and that I should never manage to be serious again.

"Well done!" said my father, his spirits rising, too. Then, with an elegant, airy gesture, he indicated the door. "Can we leave now?"

The guide took another drink.

"Too much," said my mother, uneasily. "Too much. If you drink too much, you'll lose your way."

114

"And if he loses it? What'll happen?" I asked with my mouth wide open as if to laugh. I wanted to cry, but I only giggled more than ever.

The plump little peasant suddenly made up his mind.

"Let's go!" he said, putting on his leather coat. He kissed his wife and gave us some instructions.

"Never walk one beside the other. Always in file, as if we weren't together. If I stop, you stop. If I lie down flat, you do the same. If I run, you run."

My father interrupted good-naturedly: "I'm sixty, my friend. It's not easy for me to run, you know."

The peasant suddenly froze. "Anyone who's running to save his life has no age," he said, tightening his belt. "On your way!"

We went out into the darkness. The guide was in front, my mother next, then me. My father brought up the rear. We kept a distance of six or eight paces apart. It was a quarter to ten, and the street was deserted. Our footsteps echoed as if we were walking under an arch. Soon we left the town and found ourselves in the vineyards. They were well-tended. But how difficult it was to walk through them! The earth was rough and slippery, and it was very dark. The guide advanced at a rapid pace and we had to keep up with him. My father stumbled and stifled a cry. The guide growled: "Silence."

My father found it difficult to walk in the dark; he kept slipping on the clods of earth. I longed to give him my arm, but we could only walk in Indian file among the vines. At last, we arrived at the foot of a hill. A stream flowed in front of us and the rain began to fall again. It protected us, for it made visibility poor. The frontier guards could see no better than we.

The darkness dissipated the effects of the alcohol. I stared at my feet and listened to the dragging sound of footsteps. I was past knowing whether I was afraid or not. The moment was beyond my grasp; events overwhelmed me, and I felt swept beyond the limits of human comprehension. I kept on walking.

The guide stopped abruptly and, with a motion of his hand, ordered us to squat. Panting, we sat on the wet grass. How good it was to rest even for a little while! It was eleven by the luminous dial of my watch.

Was it possible we had already been walking for an hour and a quarter? The sweat began to chill my back. I was thirsty.

The guide approached us without raising himself upright.

"I don't know if they've already passed," he whispered, and added: "I'm afraid."

It was more irritating than alarming to hear him say he was afraid. What must we be feeling if *he* was afraid? We lay down in the soaking grass. The main road ran not far from us, the cement showing pale and smooth in the darkness. It was agonizing to know that we would have to cross that broad, clear gap. How much longer would we have to wait? The distant blast of a whistle broke the silence. Some minutes later, a car passed by. The shape of the guide reared up again.

"They've gone," he said. "We can try to get across."

"Is the road the frontier?" I asked him.

He underlined his impatience with a little shake of his head. "Of course not. The frontier is still a long way off."

Where was the frontier? What was the frontier like? We reached the edge of the road. The road grew wider before our eyes as if being spread out by an invisible hand.

"Run!" ordered our guide.

My parents crossed the highway as if it were a skating rink. They tried to run but all they could do was stumble. We were in the middle. An inner force urged me to be quick, but I kept pace with my parents. The guide, who had already reached the other side, gesticulated and cursed.

"At last!" he said, when we arrived. "Now there's a clearing, then the forest begins."

The road stretched behind us like a silver ribbon. We ran through the clearing and finally reached the trees. I leaned against the first damp trunk to catch my breath, pressing my face against the bark.

The guide never stopped grumbling: "This is the last time I do this job with old people. It's impossible. They creep along like snails."

We continued on our way, plunging into dead leaves up to our ankles. It was very dark. From time to time, a wet branch brushed against my face. And it was then, suddenly, during that crazy journey, that I realized to whom that nameless mouth and that caressing hand belonged.

To Pista. I saw him again as I had seen him one day when he had said something to me, very close to the candle. I did not remember what he said but I could see his mouth and the gleam of his splendid white teeth. And the hand belonged to him, too, the hand that had helped me across the plank above the drowned man. It was then he had stroked my cheek. I only realized it at that moment. Yes, at that very moment he was near me. He was holding my hand.

"Lie down," hissed the guide. "Lie down."

We were lying full-length in the leaves but I no longer felt so abandoned. Pista was there helping me to overcome these last difficulties. The guide ordered us to go on. All I heard

118

was his authoritative voice; all I felt was the contact of the wet soil; it was so dark that I could see nothing. The labored panting of the two tormented, older people hardly reached me. We walked on, making an agonizing effort, and I had not the strength even to glance at my watch.

The forest was growing less dense; the guide was becoming more and more uneasy and hostile.

"You'll have to pay more. For old people like you, I shall charge extra."

"You shall have all you want, but get us across the frontier," said my father. His voice seemed very far away, yet he was only a couple of steps from me.

A clearing, then, suddenly, the moon began to shine with all its brilliance, with all its celestial coldness. Our guide started to swear again, but I no longer paid the least attention to him. Water was running down my neck, my hair was soaked, and my damp clothes imprisoned me like armor. The dazzling moonlight flooded the black landscape.

"That's the frontier," growled the guide. "And that infernal moon has to shine! We'll have to run. Go on, run, even if it kills you!"

Why had I always believed that a frontier must, of necessity, be a physical obstacle? A barrier — like a wall along a mountain road. Then I saw, as I ran, stupefied and sobbing with the effort, that the frontier was only black grass and moonlight. I walked in the light as if drowned in a silver bath, and there where it shone most intensely, there where my hand and my hair and my heart were whitest — there lay the frontier.

I swathed myself in those enchanted rays.

After the clearing, darkness suddenly came on us, and I heard the voice of the guide, relaxed now: "You can sit down; we're in no man's land."

I collapsed beside my parents. I pressed one cheek against the earth, against this earth which belonged to no one and which was mine. This was where I was at home: here where spirits met again in the luminous void that stretched between the two halves of the world.

"Let's go on," said the man, after a brief rest.

We were walking on Austrian soil. But the station we had to reach was still a long way off. My mother took off her shoes and wrapped her feet in a silk scarf which she had torn in two. She walked the rest of the way like that. My father stumbled along, but his courage remained unshaken.

Dawn found us in a little Austrian station. Street hawkers and men in short leather breeches occupied the waiting room. They spoke a language I did not understand. It was the first time that I had ever been in a foreign country. If I were to speak, people would look at me with astonishment. Our guide withdrew with my father; when he returned, he shook hands with us.

"You're in luck. Now you're safe. Your train to Vienna leaves in ten minutes."

And, after this farewell, he disappeared into the crowd.

Now we were alone once more. My mother put on her shoes and I, I had an inexpressible longing for a cup of boiling hot coffee.

"I bought two thousand Austrian schillings from him," explained my father. "He let me have them at a fair rate of exchange and he's bought our tickets to Vienna. A very decent fellow! I only hope he gets home without a hitch."

I asked: "How long will those two thousand schillings last?"

My father considered.

"About two months. At least, I hope so."

"And, after that, what will become of us?"

"After that, we shall have to begin life all over again. . . ."

The waiting room became more and more animated. The women packed their big baskets and bustled onto the platform. We, whose limbs were numb, dragged ourselves along like half-conscious survivors of a shipwreck, who, after a struggle with the undertow, reach dry land with their last breath.

Stiff with sleep, we managed to sit upright

on the wooden benches of the little local train. A sullen conductor punched our tickets with complete indifference. Opposite me, a man lit his pipe with ritual care. The nauseating smell of cheap tobacco turned my stomach. It began to rain again. The landscape melted into the gray sky. In the distance, factory chimneys passed, then ruins, and still more ruins. I felt I had been on this train for years, as if fate had nailed me to this hard, wooden seat and forced me to travel unceasingly past endless ruins, in the company of silent beings. I had believed that, beyond the frontier, beyond Hungary, in the countries they called Western, the sky would be blue and the people happy. That they would surround us joyfully and that their smile of welcome would make us forget the past. But in the train nobody smiled at all and the tobacco smoke became thicker and more and more unbearable.

We were approaching Vienna. I looked avidly out of the window. My heart beat fast. How many times had my parents talked to me of that enchanted city, always sparkling with gaiety? The train stopped in the midst of ruins. It had to be the station, since everyone was getting out. We, too, got out. The rain trickled down the charred walls and dripped off the broken gutters. In a few seconds we were soaked to the skin. The crowd swept us along toward the exit. My coat became heavier and heavier, and I wanted to tear off the cocoon of wretched clothes I had worn for three days. Suddenly I felt the pins that held my nightgown give way. Impossible to stop it from unrolling its full length! There I stood with the rain pouring down my face onto my gray coat from which protruded several inches of silk nightgown. I felt impotent and ridiculous. The light blue contrasted so sharply with the dingy gray that it began to attract stares. People stopped and looked at me without the faintest smile.

In tears, I ran toward a nearby hut. The nightgown hindered my progress, clinging to my ankles; the muddy water soaked through my shoes and splashed my clothes. When, at last, I got under cover, I had to wait until my hands stopped trembling. At first I wanted to tear the silk that had appeared at such an awkward moment, but the material resisted. It was stronger than I. There was no other solution but to pin it up again. At last I was able to join my parents and we left the station. The curtain of rain blocked our view. Where, oh where, was Vienna?

We set off, walking at random. Chance brought us to the doors of a cafe, we went in. The waiter gave us one glance and resumed his chat with a customer. At another table, a couple was drinking coffee. The man occasionally spoke a few words; the woman never answered.

We sat down. The waiter came up and flicked a duster over the table.

"Three coffees and something to eat," my father said in German.

We were so utterly exhausted that we could find nothing to say to each other. Sitting motionless, we looked out at the street where the wind was making the rain swirl. A stout old lady pushed open the door and entered, carrying a very fat dachshund in her arms. That reminded me of our dog. Perhaps he was still running desperately in pursuit of the train and of his faith in human beings.

The waiter brought us coffee and three small gray rolls. I bent over the cup, closed my eyes and drank. The beverage was coffee in name only, but it was scalding and it warmed both body and heart. Already, the street seemed less hostile. I devoured one of the little rolls. At that moment, I caught sight of myself in the mirror opposite and I noticed that I was smiling.

"We've succeeded," murmured my father.

He asked for the bill and drew out a hundred schilling note, which he laid on the table. The waiter came up and scrutinized the note, without touching it.

"It's out of date," he said. "All the money you've got there was withdrawn from circulation over a year ago. It's no longer worth anything at all."

My heart began to beat so violently that each throb gave me a sharp pain, like a wound. My mother was horrified; my father turned pale. We stared at the schillings on the table.

The waiter become hostile. "D'you mean you have nothing to pay for your drinks?"

His voice had become shrill, like a woman's voice. The man at the next table put down his newspaper and watched the scene, leaning on his elbows. The taciturn couple turned around, also the woman with the dog.

My mother removed her ring, her only ring, the ring that had never left her and that she had worn ever since her marriage on the same finger with her wedding ring. A blue spark flashed from the diamond, like a cry of distress. My mother handed the ring to the waiter.

"This is for the coffee. We didn't know that our money was no good."

The waiter took the ring with mistrust.

"It's not a false stone?"

But the diamond sparkled so brilliantly that no more was needed to convince him.

"Don't give it to him," I implored my mother in Hungarian.

"We must, however," said my father. "God

knows what may happen if he exposes us. We have just arrived illegally and our papers are not in order."

"We'll come and redeem it," said my mother to the waiter.

The man nodded but, from that moment, we realized that he had made up his mind never to recognize us and to deny everything if we ever did return.

He thoughtfully held the ring in his palm. Then he tossed it in the air, caught it, and thrust it into his pocket.

As he cleared away the cups, he said: "You've only just arrived, haven't you?" Then he withdrew to the far end of the dining room.

"And now what?" I asked in despair.

My parents were silent. In those five minutes they had aged several years.

I wanted to burst into sobs but my eyes remained dry.

And I wondered, in the innermost depths of my being, whether one day life would have pity on me, whether it would consent, at last, that I should have an existence of my own.

How good that would be, to be born.